SEE YOU IN COURT!

HOW TO CONDUCT YOUR OWN CASE IN THE SMALL CLAIMS COURT

SEE YOU IN COURT!

HOW TO CONDUCT YOUR OWN CASE IN THE SMALL CLAIMS COURT

Anthony Reeves

RIGHT WAY

Typeset in 11/12½pt Times by Letterpart Limited.
Printed and bound in Great Britain by Cox & Wyman Ltd., Reading, Berkshire.

The *Right Way* series is published by Elliot Right Way Books, Brighton Road, Lower Kingswood, Tadworth, Surrey, KT20 6TD, U.K. For information about our company and the other books we publish, visit our web site at www.right-way.co.uk

CONTENTS

CHAPTER   PAGE
Preface   7
 1   What is the "Small Claims Court"?   10
 2   Checking the Law and Deciding the Merits
       of Your Claim   18
 3   What to do Before Starting Court Action   31
 4   Starting Court Action   49
 5   Serving the Claim and the Defendant's Reply   65
 6   Your Opponent's Reply and Responding
       to a Defence   79
 7   The Court Hearing   92
 8   Enforcing Judgment   106
 9   Alternatives to Court Action   121
10   Making a Claim Before the Civil Justice Reforms   134
Appendix A: Official Forms   137
Appendix B: Summons (pre-reform)   149
Appendix C: Fees   154
Appendix D: Useful Addresses and Contacts   155
Index   159

DEDICATION

This book is dedicated to "Haggis".

Many thanks to Karen for reading the early drafts and
suggesting improvements.

ACKNOWLEDGEMENTS

Crown copyright is reproduced with the permission of the
Controller of Her Majesty's Stationery Office.

PREFACE

To the ordinary lay person, the thought of conducting a legal case by himself may be a daunting prospect. The main purpose of the small claims procedure of the County Court is to enable the lay person to bring his own claim. The rules are simplified and the cases come to court more quickly. The hearing, known as an arbitration, is very informal without all the complex rules of evidence. The judge has the power to conduct the arbitration in whatever way he feels is suitable and will intervene to help the claimant to present his case in the best possible way.

The purpose of this book is to explain how to make a small claim. It deals with the law and procedure for claims that come within the jurisdiction of England and Wales. There is a separate legal system in Scotland. Therefore, this book does not deal with claims that come within the jurisdiction of the Scottish legal system.

There are many situations which may result in court action. These days, people are more prepared to complain if they feel they have received a poor deal. This may be a disgruntled shopper who has been sold faulty goods, or a holidaymaker who was promised a luxury hotel when the reality was a half built ruin. It may be a motorist who has been in an accident which was not his fault and wants to recover his losses.

This book does not set out every type of legal claim that could enter the small claims procedure. Instead, it focuses on a few cases of the kind that frequently arise and provides case studies to illustrate the law and each step of the court procedure. Also, this book does not give a comprehensive statement of the law. Only the basic legal principles are explained.

The chapters dealing with the stages before court action are very important. Learning to understand the issues involved, negotiating and writing an effective letter will mean you rarely become involved in court action. It should always be your intention to settle a claim without court action. Although this book encourages the ordinary person to pursue a small claim if appropriate, remember that a court does not like a "vexatious litigant" – someone who constantly brings frivolous cases to court. A court can take action to stop a vexatious litigant.

Cases are referred to the small claims procedure when the claim involves £5,000 or less. The limit was raised to £5,000 in line with the proposals in The Woolf Report. Some cases will have started under the old system. If your case began before the new rules took effect, then you should read Chapter 10 which outlines the old system.

With the increase in the arbitration limit, the small claims court has grown in significance. The number of claims that enter the procedure will increase. People are discovering that it has become easier to sue for a small debt. In fact, with the "no costs" rule it is not economic to instruct a solicitor. There are some legal expenses policies which cover small claims but they usually have a restriction that they only cover the writing of letters and not the issuing of court action. The parties can be represented by a solicitor at the arbitration but the courts prefer lawyers to be involved only if there is a need for representation. This may be where a party is at some disadvantage, for example he has a serious speech impediment. If cases involve complicated facts or difficult points of law, then the matter would not follow the small claims procedure and the winner would be able to claim his legal costs.

With the right preparation, most arbitrations can be handled without a lawyer. However, before you begin your claim, it would be advisable to check to see if you have understood the legal issues involved by attending one of the many free legal surgeries offered by solicitors.

Whilst every effort has been made to ensure that this book provides accurate and expert guidance, it is impossible to predict every situation that may arise. Therefore, the author, publisher and retailer cannot be held liable for any loss or damage caused by the information or any mistake contained in this book.

The author regrets that he is not able to enter into correspondence concerning the material in this book. If the reader has doubts over the particular facts of a case he is pursuing, then he should seek legal advice.

When referring to the hypothetical person, the masculine ''he'' is used but this is intended to include ''she''.

1

WHAT IS THE "SMALL CLAIMS COURT"?

- Introduction
- The County Court
- When are Cases Allocated to the Small Claims Procedure?

Introduction

The "small claims court" is the common name given to a procedure within the County Court where defended cases with a value below a certain level are dealt with by arbitration. Arbitration is an informal hearing of a case where the strict rules of evidence do not apply. An arbitration is conducted by a District Judge in one of his private rooms known as "chambers". The purpose of the small claims court is to provide the opportunity for the lay person to sue for a small amount of money using a procedure that is simplified and relatively speedy. The hearing is informal to suit non-lawyers. As the procedure is simplified, it takes less time to arrive at a hearing date from the moment court action is started.

The small claims court originated in 1973. At that time, cases were referred to the small claims procedure if a defended claim was for £500 or less. This limit subsequently rose to £1,000. Following the interim report on the civil justice system by Lord Woolf, the small claim limit was raised to £3,000 in 1996. With the full implementation of the Woolf reforms, the small claims limit increased to £5,000. The recent reforms created a system of three tracks within the County Court. The multi track and fast track are new procedures but the small claims track is simply the new name for the small claims procedure.

When a defence is entered in a claim that has a value of not more than £5,000, the case is normally referred to the small claims procedure. Claims that are not specifically for a sum of money may also be allocated to the small claims procedure. Also, claims for compensation for personal injuries below £1,000 can be dealt with through the small claims procedure. When a defendant does not respond to a claim with a value within the small claims limit, it is not allocated to the small claims procedure. In this situation, you would request judgment to be entered in default. The procedures for this and other situations where a defendant does not enter a defence are explained in Chapter 5.

The County Court
In England and Wales there are around 300 County Courts. The County Court deals with civil cases. Civil actions concern disputes that are not concerned with the criminal law. Magistrates and Crown Courts hear criminal cases. Often, County Courts are situated in the same buildings as the local Magistrates Court.

Each County Court has administrative staff who work in the court office under the supervision of the Chief Clerk. The court office staff deal with all the administration of a court case. They can advise the parties on the necessary forms to complete but they cannot give legal advice. The theory behind the recent increase in court fees was to make cases more self-financing and so enable the courts to provide a more efficient service. The Court Service is responsible for the running of the County Courts. It operates a customer charter with a guide to expected standards of service. However, the level of service you receive tends to vary around the country.

The County Courts have district judges who are appointed

by the Lord Chancellor from solicitors of 7 years' standing. It
is the district judges who hear small claims.

When are Cases Allocated to the Small Claims Procedure?

The County Court is comprised of three tracks:

- The multi track for claims with a value that is larger than £15,000.
- The fast track for claims that have a value between £5,000 and £15,000.
- The small claims track for claims that have a value of £5,000 or less.

Where a defendant files a defence to a claim, the court will
serve an allocation questionnaire. The court will allocate the
claim to a track when the defendant files the allocation
questionnaire. The small claims track is the normal track for:

- A claim with a financial value of not more than £5,000.
- A claim for personal injury with a financial value of not more than £1,000.
- A housing disrepair claim relating to residential premises brought by the tenant against his landlord where the cost of the work in question is not more than £1,000.

The general rule regarding allocation is that the court will
allocate to the normal track for that claim. So a claim for not
more than £5,000 will normally be allocated to the small
claims track unless the court considers that another track is
more suitable having regard to:

- The financial value.
- The nature of the remedy sought.
- The likely complexity of the facts, law or evidence.
- The number of parties involved.
- The value and complexity of any counterclaim.

- The amount of oral evidence which may be required.
- The importance of the claim to persons who are not parties to the proceedings.
- The views expressed by the parties.
- The circumstances of the parties.

In deciding the financial value of a claim, the rules disregard any claim for interest, costs and any contributory negligence. The allocation questionnaire provides each party with an opportunity to say if he objects to the case being in the small claims procedure. Where a claim is not for a specified sum, the court will use the above factors to decide the appropriate track.

A small claim may not be automatically referred to arbitration where there is a difficult point of law and it would be more appropriate for the case to be heard by a higher court with experienced judges. Also, such a situation may involve a point of law that has not been considered by a higher court or the case may have far reaching implications.

The case study involving Export Link Ltd and Upmarket Housing Association is the type of case that a district judge may decide has a complex point of law or fact and so should not be referred to the small claims procedure.

Case Study 1. Export Link Ltd and Upmarket Housing Association

Export Link Ltd is a company which designs and sells software. Upmarket Housing's I.T. department purchase software for their new office computer system. The contract contains an exclusion clause which states that damage caused by defective software does not cover viruses that may or may not be in the program. Upmarket Housing Association use the software and later discover a virus in their computer system. It costs Upmarket Housing Association £4,000 to repair the damage caused to their computer network. Upmarket argue that the software from Export Link contained the virus. They also argue that as they bought the software as a consumer and not in the course of business, the exclusion clause is invalid because it attempts to restrict liability for a defective product. Export Link argue that their software did not contain the virus and, even if it did, Upmarket Housing Association purchased the software in the course of business and so the exclusion clause would only be invalid if it fails the reasonableness test, which they believe it does not.

The district judge is likely to cancel the reference to the small claims procedure in the case of Export Link. There is a difficult question of law concerning the validity of an exclusion clause (see Chapter 2 for the law relating to unfair contract terms and exclusion clauses). It is likely that a court would decide that Upmarket Housing bought the software as a business and not a consumer. However, that would still leave the question of whether or not the exclusion clause, which attempts to exclude liability, is reasonable. Also, the question of whether or not the software caused the virus to enter Upmarket's computer system could be a difficult issue of fact. These difficult points of law and fact would be better decided at a full trial.

The automatic reference to the small claims procedure would not always be cancelled if the defendant had a counter-claim that was larger than the arbitration limit. It is only one of the factors which the district judge considers.

Most of the claims that are referred to arbitration will not be as complicated as the case study involving Export Link Ltd and Upmarket Housing Association. Typical claims in the small claims procedure concern:

- Simple debt actions, e.g. claims for unpaid bills.
- Consumer claims, e.g. claims in respect of faulty goods or bad service.
- Road traffic accidents, e.g. cost of repairs or insurance policy excess.
- Claims for the return of deposits by former tenants.

A typical debt action is where goods and services have been

provided but payment remains outstanding. A wide variety of consumer claims enter the small claims procedure. A claim in respect of faulty goods is just one common example: you may have purchased new electrical goods, for example, and a few weeks later they fail to work. Claiming losses arising from road accidents is another common type of small claim. This might be a policy excess, repairs to your vehicle or hire car charges while your car is off the road. An increasing number of claims concern tenants and their landlords. Tenants may experience difficulty in obtaining the return of deposits. In other cases, the tenant may have a claim against the landlord because he fails to fulfil his obligation under the tenancy to keep the property in reasonable repair.

Claims that are not specifically for an amount of money can be referred to the small claims procedure. So a claim for specific performance will be referred to arbitration provided its value is below the small claims limit. Specific performance is when you are asking the court to order the defendant to perform what was agreed in a contract. An example of a claim for specific performance is given in case study 2 involving Graham and Julie.

Case Study 2. Graham and the purchase of a VW Beetle
Graham sees a VW Beetle advertised privately in his local paper. He is excited by the advert as he has been looking for this model for a long time. He rings the telephone number given and arranges with Julie, the seller, to view it. Julie lets Graham take the car for a test drive and he decides to make her an offer of £2,500. Julie accepts the offer and Graham decides to pay a deposit of £75 as she says there is a lot of interest in the car. Julie gives Graham a receipt for the deposit stating it relates to the sale of the VW Beetle. Graham says he will return the next day and pay the balance of the price with a banker's draft. When Graham returns the next day, Julie says she has decided not to sell the VW Beetle and gives his deposit back. Graham is extremely disappointed as it was the car he wanted. Graham tells Julie that he believed there was an

enforceable contract and says he will take the matter to court.

The facts indicate that there was an enforceable contract between Graham and Julie. Graham made an offer to buy the car for £2,500 which Julie accepted. This is supported by the fact that Graham paid a deposit and obtained a receipt which stated it was in respect of the sale of the car. If Graham made a claim, it would be asking the court for the remedy of specific performance. This would be a judgment which orders Julie to fulfil the contract and sell the car to Graham. If Julie entered a defence, although it is difficult to see what that could be, the case would be referred to the small claims procedure even though it was not a money claim.

If a claim is for personal injury then it would be referred to the small claims procedure provided the damages that could be awarded for the pain and suffering are £1,000 or less. In reality, very few claims involving personal injury are likely to be heard in the small claims court. This is because the injury would have to be very minor to be awarded £1,000 or less. An example would be a neck injury giving rise to symptoms for only a couple of weeks. This might be caused by whiplash in a road traffic accident, where the person suffers only minor aches and pains for the couple of weeks and then makes a full recovery. Courts decide the level of compensation for personal injuries by reference to earlier cases with similar injuries. The Judicial Studies Board publishes guidelines stating the range of compensation for particular injuries. This booklet is a good starting point for deciding the amount of compensation you might receive for a personal injury. It is so well respected that judges in court refer to it. It gives lawyers the broad range in which a particular injury falls and then they look at specific cases to get a more precise figure of compensation.

If an injury is very minor, then a person may decide that it is not worth seeking compensation. Another reason why the small claims procedure handles few claims for minor personal injuries is that they involve additional procedural requirements. When you start a claim for personal injury, you need to attach a medical report to the particulars of claims. If the personal injury claim is only a few hundred pounds for a sprained ankle, then it may not be worth obtaining a medical report. Even if you only obtain a short letter from your G.P., he will charge you a fee.

2

CHECKING THE LAW AND DECIDING THE MERITS OF YOUR CLAIM

- Introduction
- The Legal Basis of Your Claim
- Applying the Law and Assessing the Merits of Your Claim

Introduction

Although the hearing of a small claim is described as an arbitration, the decision is made by applying the general law to the facts of the dispute. Many small claims arise out of contracts, especially contracts for the supply of goods or services. A large number arise out of road accidents when the question of fault is decided according to the law of tort. Tort is concerned with a civil wrong, which gives the plaintiff the right to bring an action in the civil courts. Some claims involve liability under statute, for example a claim against a highway authority for a failure to maintain the highway.

It is important that you understand the basic principles of the law relating to your claim. Although you may not be instructing a solicitor to conduct your claim, it may be worth taking advantage of the free legal surgeries which most solicitors operate. Alternatively, you could visit your local citizens advice bureau.

The first part of this chapter outlines the general law in the areas that frequently arise in small claims. It is not a detailed statement of the law, but provides the general principles. The second part illustrates how the merits of a claim are determined by applying the relevant law to the facts of a case.

The Legal Basis of Your Claim
The areas of law most likely to be encountered are:

- negligence
- contract.

Negligence is the basis of a claim arising from a road traffic accident. A breach of contract is the basis of most consumer claims. A claim for a simple debt is a claim for a breach of contract, for example an unpaid invoice when goods have been sold and delivered under a contract.

Negligence
The basic definition of negligence is the failure to do what the reasonable man would do, or doing something which a reasonable man would not do.

There are three elements to proving negligence:

i.   a duty of care
ii. that the duty has been breached (or not matched up to the standard expected) and
iii. that breach of duty has caused the damage or loss.

i.   First, the defendant must owe a duty of care to the plaintiff. In the case of the driver of a vehicle, the law states that a driver owes a duty of care to other road users. This means that he is under a legal obligation to take into account other road users when driving his vehicle. The example of driving is a good way of explaining the principle of a duty of care but the law has created many other situations where a person must consider those around him when he acts or fails to act in some way.

ii.   The second aspect of negligence is to decide whether the duty of care has been breached. The mythical "reasonable man" appears on many occasions in English law. The standard of the reasonable man is based on that of the ordinary decent citizen. This reasonable man is neither careless nor overly careful. What is appropriate depends on the circumstances and what the reasonable man would have done (or not have done). In the case of a driver, you are expected to drive as the reasonably competent driver would. A reasonably competent driver is not expected, for example, to pull out of a junction unless it is safe to do so. The Highway Code provides a good guide to what is expected of the reasonable driver. In the case of road traffic accidents, deciding who is at fault is often a matter of common sense.

iii. The third aspect is whether the act or failure to act caused the resulting damage or loss. If the damage would not have happened but for a particular fault, then that fault is the cause of the damage. If it would have happened just the same, fault or no fault, the fault is not the cause of the damage.

Contract

A contract is an agreement between two parties which is intended to have legal consequences. A contract can be made verbally or in writing. The obvious problem with an oral contract is that it can be difficult to prove the terms of the agreement. Some contracts have to be in writing to be valid, such as contracts for the sale of land. There are various elements of a contract but it is not necessary to examine them in detail. You need, however, to understand that a contract can have express and implied terms. An express term is a term that is written in the contract. Sometimes a term of the contract may not actually be written in the agreement but is implied due to statute, common law or custom.

Contracts for the sale of goods contain a number of basic terms which are implied by statute. The Sale of Goods Act 1979 (as amended)[1] implies into a contract:

- that the goods are of satisfactory quality,
- that the goods belong to the person selling them,
- that they fit their description and
- they are fit for the purpose for which they are sold.

These implied terms apply where the consumer buys from a trader. Second hand goods are covered but you cannot expect the same standard as if they were new goods. They do not apply to a private sale. So when you buy from a private individual and something goes wrong with the product, unless there has been a misrepresentation, the seller has no responsibility. If, however, someone advertises goods for sale and pretends to be a private seller when really they are a trader, then that is a criminal offence. Advertisements must make it clear when goods are being sold in the course of a business.

Other statutes imply terms into contracts. The Supply of Goods and Services Act 1982 applies to anyone providing a service which involves materials. This would cover the builder or garage mechanic conducting repairs to a vehicle. This Act implies the following terms into a contract:

- the person providing the service should exercise reasonable care and skill,
- the service will be carried out within a reasonable time,
- the materials used should be fit for the purpose and be of satisfactory quality,
- if no price is mentioned, a reasonable price will be paid.

---

[1] The Sale and Supply of Goods Act 1994 amended the implied term as to quality.

Unfair Contract Terms

A contract for the supply of goods or services may contain provisions which attempt to restrict or remove the rights of the consumer. The customer may challenge such provisions as unfair and therefore invalid. The terms may be regarded as unfair under the Unfair Terms in Consumer Contracts Regulations or the Unfair Contract Terms Act 1977. The implied terms mentioned above cannot be excluded. If a clause states that the contract does not include the implied terms as to quality, it would not be valid. So, for example, if a consumer buys goods from a shop which has a notice ''no refunds'' then that type of exclusion clause will not usually be allowed under the Unfair Contract Terms Act. As a consumer, if the goods were faulty or did not match the description, then you would be entitled to a refund. This type of exclusion clause may be allowed in a contract between two businesses if it is reasonable.

Misrepresentation

In the negotiations leading up to a contract, a statement (representation) may be made which is not a binding contractual term. If the statement is untrue it may be a ''misrepresentation'' and can result in the contract being cancelled or a claim for compensation. A misrepresentation is:

● an untrue statement of fact, made by one party to the other, that induces the other party to enter into the contract.

If there was a misrepresentation, the remedy depends on the type of misrepresentation. It may be an innocent, negligent or fraudulent misrepresentation. It is important not to confuse sales talk with a misrepresentation. Statements such as ''this car goes like a bomb'' is mere sales talk, whereas saying the car will go more than 100 mph could amount to a misrepresentation if it is untrue.

Case Study 3. Misrepresentation: Karen and her sports car
Karen decides to buy a sports car that goes more than 100 mph
to race off road. After being assured by the garage that it goes
in excess of 120 mph, she decides to buy the car. On racing the
car at Castle Combe race track, she discovers it won't go more
than 90 mph.

Karen has a claim for misrepresentation. There was an
untrue statement of fact which induced her to enter into the
contract to buy the sports car. If, however, she would have still
entered into the contract despite the untrue statement, then it
would not be a misrepresentation because it did not induce the
agreement.

Misrepresentation is often a factor when holiday makers
complain that their holiday did not live up to expectations. A
common situation is when you book accommodation and ask
for a hotel near the sea or some particular location, but it turns
out to be a long distance away.

In reality, a misrepresentation is not easy to prove. It is
often a case of trying to prove what exactly was said. This is
not always easy if there are no records of the conversations.

Warranty Claims
Many consumer claims involve some form of warranty. A
warranty is a promise by a manufacturer (or retailer) as to the
extent they will repair, replace or otherwise compensate for
defective goods. Most new products carry a manufacturer's
warranty for the first year. Any form of warranty is in addition
to a consumer's statutory rights. This means that a warranty is
not instead of the implied terms as to quality contained in the
Sale of Goods Act which have been explained earlier in this
chapter. Warranties are useful when you have had goods for a
long time and your statutory rights no longer have effect.
Suppose you have had your new car for 11 months and a part
fails to operate, such as a starter motor. In such a case, you
should consult the warranty (if there is one) and see if the part
will be replaced under the policy. The problem with warranties, however, is that they usually contain many exclusions

which restrict their effectiveness. Often there are vague terms such as "parts will not be replaced if the defect was caused by wear and tear". Or it might require you to have met certain conditions, such as having had the car serviced at a nominated garage. Therefore, these exclusion clauses may allow the warranty companies to avoid paying.

Consumer Credit Act 1974

The Consumer Credit Act 1974 regulates the provision of consumer credit to individuals. This Act contains a number of sections which you should bear in mind when making a small claim. Section 75 may be relevant if you are considering making a claim for misrepresentation or breach of contract, where goods were purchased with a loan from a finance company or a credit card. If the finance company and the trader are not one and the same person, then, if you are making a claim against the trader (supplier of goods) for misrepresentation or breach of contract, there is a like claim against the finance company or credit card company. This means that they are jointly and severally liable, so you can sue either of them or both. Section 75 of the Consumer Credit Act is useful where the supplier of the goods may not be financially sound. Suppose you purchased goods with your credit card and on delivery they were defective. You have a claim against the credit card company as well as the supplier of the goods, so if you discover that the supplier is insolvent, you would be able to make a claim against the credit card company.

The Consumer Credit Act only applies where:

- the cash price of the goods is greater than £100 but less than £30,000 and
- the credit does not exceed £15,000 excluding interest.

Claims Under Statute

Acts of Parliament may lay down duties and obligations on organisations and individuals. An example is the Highways Act 1980 which sets out the obligations a highway authority is under to repair and maintain the roads. It is useful to look in more detail at this statute, because at a time when there are more vehicles on the road and local authorities are facing budget restrictions, there is a growth in the number of small claims arising from cars being driven into potholes. Many claims are brought by individuals tripping over dangerous paving stones, but the small claims procedure only deals with personal injury claims up to the value of £1,000.

Under the Highways Act 1980, a highway authority has a duty to maintain a highway. This applies to a public highway (a highway maintainable at public expense). The authority is required to maintain and repair it to a reasonable standard so that it is free from danger to all users who use the highway in the way normally to be expected of them. As is often the case in law, the standard is one of reasonableness. You cannot expect the highway to be in a perfect condition. It only needs to be in a reasonable condition taking into account the traffic expected to use it.

Even if you can show that the highway was in a dangerous condition, a highway authority has a statutory defence which may allow it to escape responsibility. To argue this defence successfully the highway authority has to prove it took all reasonable steps, in the circumstances, to ensure that the highway was free from hazards.

Applying the Law and Assessing the Merits of Your Claim

By this point you should have an outline of the areas of law on which your claim may be based. It is now a matter of applying the law to the facts.

In road traffic claims it is often obvious who was at fault. There is not usually any doubt in cases of a rear end shunt. The driver behind is almost always the party responsible because the reasonable driver is expected to keep a safe distance to enable him to pull up in time should the vehicle in front slow down or stop. There are other accidents where deciding fault is more difficult, for example where two vehicles collide on a bend in a narrow country lane without markings. If there were no witnesses, then consider:

- the nature of the impact,
- the resting position of each vehicle and
- whether or not there are any skid marks on the road surface.

In such accidents, take photographs before the vehicles are moved. It is a useful tip to keep a cheap disposable camera in the glove compartment. If you have accurate measurements of any skid marks then a calculation of the vehicle's speed is possible. If there are no witnesses or any photographs before the vehicles were moved, then it may be difficult to establish fault as it is one driver's word against the other. As there is usually no independent evidence with an accident on a remote road, fault is often split between the parties. In apportioning fault, the court uses a concept known as "contributory negligence". This is where the claimant is careless to his own safety or interests, which makes the damages he suffered worse. When giving judgment, a judge would say that . . . "I find the defendant negligent but there was contributory negligence on the part of the plaintiff and therefore I reduce the plaintiff's compensation by X%."

Witnesses

Evidence from an independent witness is very useful in a road traffic claim. In many instances, people are not prepared to get involved, but if they are, take their names and addresses. A witness should only give an account of what he saw. As a general rule, a witness should not give opinions. However, there are exceptions to this, for example evidence as to the speed of a vehicle. This would be permitted because it is evidence of facts personally seen by the witness. A witness must not state an opinion as to who is at fault. That is for the court to decide on hearing the evidence.

Once you have the details of the witness, contact him and

ask for a written account of what he saw. It is important to
have a written statement because memories fade with time.
Also, ask him if he would be prepared to give evidence at a
hearing should it come to that. If the witness is not able to
attend the hearing then the judge may allow the written
statement as evidence. However, not much weight would be
attached to the statement if he does not attend because the
other party does not have the opportunity to ask the witness
questions. (N.B. The judge can conduct the hearing in a
manner he feels is appropriate. This is examined later in
Chapter 7.)

A witness statement (in a road traffic accident) should
include:

- his name and address,
- where he was in relation to the accident,
- an account of what he saw without stating opinions,
- a signature and date.

If the police attended the scene they may have compiled a
report. If so you can write to their local administration unit and
ask for a copy. They will charge to send a copy of the report
(see Appendix C). A full police report can be very useful,
especially if the officers attended before the vehicles were
moved. It will usually contain statements from all of those
involved in the accident. (A copy of the police report will not
be released until any pending criminal prosecutions have been
heard.)

Assessing the Merits of a Consumer Claim
Many consumer claims involve defective goods or complaints
about the standard of workmanship. How do you assess
whether the goods you purchased were of satisfactory quality
when they subsequently fail to work? How do you judge
whether work has been carried out with reasonable care and
skill?

If you purchase a new product and it fails to work within a

few days, then you can be fairly sure that it was not of satisfactory quality. If the goods fail to work after a longer period, such as four or five months, then the issue is not so clear. The actual definition of 'satisfactory quality' is contained in section 1 of the Sale and Supply of Goods Act 1994. This act made changes to the Sale of Goods Act 1979. Before the changes, goods were required to be of 'merchantable quality'. This caused problems because there was little reference to what 'merchantable quality' actually meant. The changes made by the 1994 Act have improved matters in favour of the consumer. Goods are of satisfactory quality if:

● they meet the standard that a reasonable person would regard as satisfactory, taking account of any description of the goods, the price (if relevant) and all other relevant circumstances.

The 1994 Act goes on to state that the quality of goods includes the following aspects:

● fitness for all the purposes for which the goods are commonly supplied,
● appearance and finish,
● freedom from minor defects,
● safety,
● durability.

On the basis of this definition, you can obviously expect new products to be of a higher quality than second hand ones. Durability is stated as a factor to be considered but it does not refer to a specific length of time. You can expect new goods to last for a reasonable time. What is reasonable will depend on the circumstances. You can expect top-of-the-range models to be of a higher standard than much cheaper ones. The introduction of a list of factors to consider in relation to quality has improved things for the consumer. However, you should not make the mistake of expecting every new product to be perfect.

When you feel that a service has not been carried out to a reasonable standard, how should you go about establishing that there has been carelessness or that faulty parts were used? The case study below illustrates what you need to do in a situation where a garage has conducted substandard work on your vehicle.

Case Study 4. Paula and the troublesome gearbox
Paula had been driving her car recently and noticed a problem changing gears and so decided to take it to her local dealer. The garage examined the car and told Paula that it needed a new clutch. The car went in for the work to be done. Paula collected the vehicle and paid the bill which came to £400 including parts and labour. The invoice showed a large labour content. Two days later, Paula is driving home from work when she notices that the clutch pedal is going lower to the floor and it is difficult to change gears. She manages to return to the garage and lets them have a look at it again. She states that she thinks there is a problem with the work they carried out. They dispute this and say that it just needs an adjustment and it will be fine. On the way home from work the next day, the problem is so bad that she cannot engage the gears and so has to be towed home by the RAC. She contacts the garage and demands that they sort out the fault without further charge. The garage refuses and argues that the work they did on the clutch was fine and that the problem is an unconnected fault inside the gearbox. Paula is convinced that the problem has been caused by the garage.

Paula's argument is that the garage did not use reasonable care and skill. She will need evidence to support her suspicions. She would be well advised to obtain an independent report. It would seem appropriate to ask the RAC to examine the vehicle to establish the cause of the fault. If it can be proved, on the balance of probabilities, that the fault was caused as a result of the garage not taking reasonable care or using faulty parts, then Paula should win her case. The report could be expensive and may not be conclusive. It could cost around £100. A cheaper alternative might be to ask a reputable local garage to examine it. If the report is favourable, a copy should be sent to the garage with a letter before action (see Chapter 3). If Paula wins her case, the judge can award a witness allowance of up to £200 for an expert report to cover the cost of preparation and attendance at the arbitration if necessary. (The details of what costs can be awarded at a small claims hearing are examined in Chapter 7 on page 103).

3

WHAT TO DO BEFORE STARTING COURT ACTION

- Negotiation
- Letters Before Action
- Alternatives to Court Action
- The Financial Circumstances of
  Your Opponent

Having taken advice on the legal merits of your claim, the next step is to attempt to settle the matter without having to start court action. If you are aware of your legal position and have arranged the facts in a coherent fashion, then efforts to negotiate a settlement are more likely to succeed. You should always consider compromising in an effort to settle your claim. If your opponent makes an offer which is close to what a court may award, you should consider it carefully. There is no guarantee that you will succeed in court and much time and effort goes into making a claim. This might persuade you to accept the offer. If attempts to settle achieve no result, then begin preparing your case in readiness for court proceedings.

Negotiation
Not every claim, or potential claim, will follow exactly the same pattern of events. It can be difficult to predict the way matters will develop. This is especially true in a consumer dispute. Sometimes you can achieve a satisfactory result in

circumstances where you were expecting the trader to be unhelpful. Other times, a trader may be awkward where you feel you are being perfectly reasonable. There are no set rules to achieving a successful negotiation. The approach you take will depend on the reaction of the other party. What is important is to prepare yourself before launching into a telephone discussion or a face-to-face meeting. The advice may sound obvious but the simple things can often increase your chances of a successful negotiation. Imagine you are about to make a telephone call to complain about faulty goods or poor workmanship. Before you pick up the telephone you should:

- Make a brief note of the facts in a logical order.
- Put into concise form the basis of your complaint, i.e. goods not of ''satisfactory quality'' or work not carried out with ''reasonable care and skill'.
- Anticipate what the other person might say and have counter-arguments prepared.

During the conversation, make a conscious effort to stick to relevant issues. Be assertive but remain polite. This might be difficult if the other party is abusive but exchanging insults is unlikely to progress matters in your favour. At the end of the conversation, remember to make a detailed note for future reference. The above points are just as relevant in a face-to-face meeting.

The previous chapter explored the main points of law relating to the types of claim that are likely to be brought in the small claims court. It is important to be aware of the legal points before starting negotiations otherwise there is a danger that you could prejudice your position. You should not be preoccupied with legal issues, but those who know the appropriate law can negotiate from a stronger position. A consumer who is not aware of his statutory rights may be at a disadvantage when trying to complain about faulty goods to a smooth talking retailer. You should not feel daunted by the points of law. The legal issues involved with claims that go to arbitration will usually be straightforward.

If they are more complicated then the district judge will refer the case out of the small claims procedure for a full trial.

"Without Prejudice" Letters

In an effort to settle a claim, you may decide to make concessions or be prepared to accept less than you are entitled to recover. If you write such a letter which makes concessions in order to reach a settlement, it is advisable to head the letter with the words "without prejudice". So, for example, if you said to the defendant ". . . in an effort to settle this claim I would accept £300 instead of the full £400", you should head the letter without prejudice or at least clearly state in the letter that the offer is without prejudice to your claim. The reason for this is that if the defendant does not settle the matter by paying the £300, you could still decide to take court action to recover the full amount. The defendant cannot use the without prejudice offer against you in court. If the other party accepts your without prejudice offer, then that is a contract and both parties are bound by it.

Without prejudice letters are often used by insurance companies who make offers close to what the claimant may accept as a way of settling the matter, particularly if they do not have a strong defence to the claim.

Negotiating a Claim Involving Faulty Goods

Case Study 5. Judy and the faulty washing machine

Judy buys a new washing machine on the 1st April for £500 from Upmarket Electricals Ltd. Three weeks later, the machine starts to make a knocking noise and won't spin at the end of the wash cycle. She rings Upmarket Electricals and an engineer comes out to have a look. The engineer mentions that there is a minor fault involving a loose connection. After the engineer's visit, the machine continues to work for a further 4 weeks and then the machine will not work at all. Judy is very angry and wants Upmarket Electricals to take the washing machine back and refund her money.

Upmarket Electricals offer to repair the machine but refuse

to take it back and refund her money.

In many of the cases involving faulty goods, especially new ones, the customer approaches the retailer and requests a refund. When you approach a reputable retailer and explain the problems you have had so soon after purchase, they are happy to refund or replace the goods in the interests of good customer relations. In such a situation, the desired result has been achieved without much effort. Of course, this will not always be the case. A response that is often received when you complain about faulty goods is that they would be happy to repair the goods without charge. Before allowing the goods to be repaired, pause to consider the following points:

● *Make it clear that by allowing repairs you are not accepting the goods.*

The Sale and Supply Goods Act 1994 states that by allowing goods to be repaired, it does not necessarily mean you are accepting the goods. However, it is still worth making it clear to the retailer that by allowing the repairs you are not accepting the goods. This is important if the goods are still faulty when they are returned. If you then decide to reject the goods, you still have the right to claim a refund. Allowing the goods to be repaired once should not prejudice your rights, but several repairs may affect your right to reject.

● *State a time scale for the repairs to be completed.*

Where the retailer offers to repair the goods, have a clear idea of when to draw the line. Try and establish how long the repairs will take. Otherwise, you have a situation where the goods are going backwards and forwards for repairs and you end up being without the goods for long periods. If the goods fail soon after being returned, then do not give the retailer another opportunity to repair.

● *Have you still got confidence in the goods?*

You should consider whether you will have confidence in the product after the repair. Spending a large amount of money on a new washing machine, as in the case of Judy, only to have it break down shortly afterwards would not make many people feel confident about the quality of the product. Therefore, when a consumer product breaks down so soon after purchase, you should nearly always refuse the offer of a free repair and demand a refund.

In the case study, Judy allowed Upmarket Electricals to repair the washing machine. After it breaks down again 4 weeks later, she has had enough and wants a refund. Although the shop has not said why they will not refund her money, it is likely that they would try and argue that Judy has had the goods for a reasonable period of time and, therefore, is deemed to have accepted the goods and cannot reject them. This is a common situation. Allowing the repair to be carried out has not affected her right to reject the machine. The point at issue is whether 7 weeks is a reasonable period of time to have had the machine without telling the seller that she wishes to reject it. The case of *Bernstein v. Pamson Motors (1987)* involved a new Nissan car whose engine seized after only 3 weeks and 140 miles of driving. It was decided that 3 weeks was a reasonable period for the buyer to have tried out the vehicle and so he was deemed to have accepted it. The decision has been criticised but the judge did say that each case depends on its own facts. So, it does not mean that a period of 3 weeks is the rule as each case depends on the circumstances. However, the sooner you tell the seller that you are rejecting faulty goods, the more likely it is that you will still have the right to return them and obtain a refund. Even if you have had the goods for too long to reject them, you could still sue for the cost of repairs if the goods were not of satisfactory quality.

Letters Before Action
If negotiations fail to resolve the dispute, then prepare a "letter before action". A letter before action should be written before court proceedings are commenced. This avoids the

other party claiming that court action was unnecessary and that payment would have been made if a letter had been written. Also, a court is likely to penalise you for not writing a letter before action. Such a letter is also a good way of assembling the facts and ensuring that you have dealt with every relevant issue. Once you have established you have a claim and the initial negotiations have failed, as in the case of Judy and the washing machine, a letter should be written. It should contain the following:

- A brief account of the relevant facts that gave rise to the claim.
- The action which you are asking the recipient to take.
- The action you will take in the event of an unsatisfactory response.
- The time limit in which you want a response.

The content of a letter before action will vary depending on the type of claim. Where the letter is to be passed to an insurer you should allow 21 days for a reply, in line with the new protocols. In a road traffic claim it is usual for the initial letter not to contain detailed allegations, as the insurers of the other driver will write requesting further information. The sample letter before action in Figure 1 contains all the important elements in the case involving Judy and the faulty washing machine: it sets out the circumstances that gave rise to her claim; it states what she requires Upmarket Electricals to do (refund her money), the time in which she wants a response and what she intends doing if her claim is not settled within that period.

Although we have considered the legal points involved, it is not necessary in the letter before action to give too much detail about the relevant law. Careful reference to the applicable law should be made in the ''particulars of claim'' that accompany the claim, assuming the case goes to court. Besides, Judy is not a lawyer and would not be expected to make a detailed reference to the law. The letter does, however, include suffi-cient reference to ''the machine not being of satisfactory quality'' to identify the legal basis on which the claim is

10 Church Street
Upmarket
Upmarketshire

The Manager
Upmarket Electricals Ltd
2 High Street
Upmarket

1st June XXXX

Dear Mr Stevens

Re: Hotspin Washing Machine

I write regarding the above washing machine which I purchased new from Upmarket Electricals Ltd on the 1st April XXXX for £500.

As I stated in our conversation yesterday, the washing machine developed a knocking noise after only 3 weeks and would not spin at the end of the wash cycle. Your engineer came out to look at it on XX/XX/XX, at which time I made it clear that by allowing the repair I was in no way accepting the goods. The washing machine was repaired and worked until the 28th May when it would not operate at all. I telephoned you immediately and stated that I was rejecting the machine and wanted a full refund.

In view of the fact that I paid £500 for a top-of-the-range model, I feel that in all the circumstances the washing machine was not of satisfactory quality and, therefore, I am entitled to reject the washing machine and claim a full refund. If I do not receive a full refund of £500 within 14 days, I shall commence proceedings in the County Court without further notice.

Yours sincerely

Miss J Howe

Figure 1. Letter before action to Upmarket Electricals from Judy in Case Study 5

founded. You will recall, from Chapter 2, that a claim in respect of faulty goods is based on a breach of the implied term in the contract that the goods should be of "*satisfactory quality*".

In a road traffic claim the letter before action should be sent to the other driver, even though you may have details of the other party's insurance company. As will be explained later, your claim is against the other driver and not the insurer, although the insurers will ultimately be the ones to pay the claim. Where you have details of the other driver's insurers, a way to speed up matters would be to send a copy of the letter direct to the insurance company.

Case Study 6. Brian and the Road Traffic Claim

Frank Smith was waiting in his Ford Capri to turn right out of the High Street and into Baker Street, in Downmarket, when his vehicle was struck by a Ford Escort (driven by Brian Jones) which was turning right into the High Street. Frank's car suffered damage to the front off side. Frank and Brian exchanged addresses plus the details of their insurance companies. Frank is insured third party, fire and theft, and claims the cost of the repairs to his vehicle which amounts to £500. Frank Smith suspects that Brian Jones will deny responsibility and claim that Frank pulled out from the junction and therefore caused the collision. According to Frank, Brian Jones cut the corner as he turned into the High Street from Baker Street. Following the accident, Frank took several photographs of the position of the vehicles before they were moved. These photographs show that Frank's car was not over the white give-way lines at the junction, indicating that Brian had cut the corner.

A letter before action in a road traffic claim should usually contain the following points:

- Time, place and location of the accident.
- The registration number of other vehicle involved.
- A brief account of what happened and that you hold the other driver responsible.

- Notice of where your vehicle is available for inspection.
- A brief statement of the losses you are claiming.
- A request that the other party pass the letter to their insurers and for the policy details if you don't already have them.
- Notice of the time limit within which you want a reply.

Figure 2 sets out a sample letter before action which Frank Smith should send to Brian Jones.

The insurers will be slow to respond to your correspondence. Don't expect their initial letter to say anything more than that they are making enquiries into the accident but in the meanwhile they want you to send more details of your claim. By "making enquiries" this means that they are probably waiting for a report to be completed by their insured. This is what sometimes causes a delay as the other driver takes a long time to return the report form. It is important not to let things drift. Make notes in your diary as a reminder to send follow up letters.

When the other party's insurers ask for further details of your claim this will either be a request for documentary evidence to support the value of your claim or more information on the allegations of negligence against their insured.

It is unlikely that an insurance company will pay a claim on the basis of a garage estimate. They usually want to see a receipted invoice after the completion of the repairs. If you are not in a position to afford to pay upfront for the repairs, then obtain a "pro-forma" invoice from the garage. A "pro-forma" invoice gives a detailed breakdown of the work to be carried out together with the parts to be used. It will show the total cost for parts and labour plus the VAT element. Most insurance companies will be prepared to make payment based on a pro-forma invoice, except for the VAT element. The VAT element will be paid once the work is completed and the final receipted invoice is presented.

When the other insurers ask for more details of the allegations of negligence they want you to be more specific about

55 Bond Street
Upmarket
UP10 2FS

Mr B Jones
44 End Terrace
Downmarket
DR11 3BJ

10th June XXXX

Dear Mr Jones

Re: Incident on 5th June XXXX, High Street, Downmarket

I write regarding the above incident on the 5th June XXXX.

At about 2pm, I was waiting to turn right from the High Street into Market Street when your Ford Escort (registration number KLW120X) collided into my vehicle causing damage. I hold you responsible for this accident due to your negligent driving in that you cut the corner as you turned right into the High Street from Market Street.

I am insured third party and therefore claim the cost of the repairs to my vehicle which is £500. (See enclosed estimates.) My vehicle is available for inspection at Upmarket Garage, Brook Street, for the next 14 days.

Please pass this letter to your insurance company. If I do not hear from you or your insurance company within the next 21 days, I will start legal proceedings in the County Court to recover my losses.

Yours sincerely

F. Smith

Figure 2. Letter before action by Frank Smith to Brian Jones

why you regard their insured as being at fault. It may be that
the information they have obtained from their insured conflicts
with your version of events. In the case study, Brian Jones
might have told his insurers that Frank Smith pulled out of the
junction as he was turning into the High Street. This is why
the photographs that Frank took, of the position of the vehicles
on impact, will be crucial evidence. Copies of these photographs should be sent to the insurers of Brian Jones. The
weakness of their insured's case will be apparent and it is
likely the claim will be settled. Whenever you send documents, photographs or letters, always keep copies.

Letters Before Action in a Highway Claim

With an increasing number of cars on the roads and a limited
budget for highway authorities to spend on repairs and maintenance, there are many more claims from motorists whose
vehicles have been damaged from driving through potholes.
Chapter 2 mentioned that highway authorities have a duty to
maintain the roads under the Highways Act 1980. The facts of
the case study concerning Susan and the damage to her car are
typical of many claims involving potholes on the highway.

Case Study 7. Highway Claim (pothole in the road)

Susan was driving her vehicle along a B road on the edge of
Upmarket when her car drove through a pothole causing
damage to the front near side wheel and suspension. The cost
of the repairs amounted to £900 plus £75 for hiring a car for
three days while her vehicle was off the road being repaired.
Susan took measurements and photographs of the pothole
which showed it to be 50cm by 30cm and 25cm deep. She
decides to make a claim against the local authority for a failure
to maintain the highway.

As was stated in Chapter 2, you cannot expect the road to be
in a perfect condition, only that it should be in a reasonable
state of repair for the type of road. However, considering the
size of the pothole, Susan has a strong argument in saying that
it is a hazard even though it is on a B road. Susan's first action

should be to write to the highway authority. Figure 3 shows the contents of Susan's letter to the highway authority.

It is important to be precise about the location of the pothole. This will enable the highway inspector to make his report more quickly. It will probably take 6 to 8 weeks before you receive a full response. Initially, you are likely to receive an acknowledgement from the local authority saying that it has been passed to their insurers. When the highway inspector has made his report, you should receive a full reply from the insurers. Figure 4 is a letter from the insurers of Upmarket County Council to Susan Hammond denying liability in respect of her claim.

It was explained in Chapter 2 that a highway authority has a defence to a claim even where the pothole was a hazard if it can show that it had taken all reasonable steps to ensure that the highway was safe. Basically, if the highway authority can show that it had a regular system of inspections appropriate for the type of road, then it can escape liability. The letter from ZMA Insurance is using this argument to deny liability.

Susan should respond by requesting to see copies of the inspection record sheet for the previous 3 years. In addition, she should ask to see the record of complaints for this particular stretch of road. She is entitled to see these documents and could apply to the court if they fail to produce them. Also, she should ask the following questions:

● How often is this particular road inspected?
● When was it last inspected and what observations did the highway inspector make?

The purpose of requesting the record sheets and asking specific questions is to see whether the highway authority has regularly inspected this area of road and in accordance with the authority's inspections policy. It will also show whether or not the highway authority had known of the pothole but had not repaired it within a reasonable time.

5 Brook Street
Upmarket
UP9 3SH

Highways Department
Upmarketshire County Council
County Hall
Upmarket

XX/XX/XX

Dear Sirs

Re: Incident on B345 Upmarket Road

I write regarding an incident that occurred on 10 July on the B345, Upmarket to Downmarket road, just north of the entrance to the Rose and Crown public house.

I was driving the vehicle when the near side wheel struck a pothole causing the car to swerve slightly. I then noticed that my steering seemed strange. On arriving in Downend I had the car examined at CC Autos. The pothole had caused damage to the wheel and suspension. I then went back and measured the pothole as being 50cm by 30cm and 25cm deep.

As a result of your failure to repair and maintain the highway under section 41 of the Highways Act 1980, I have suffered a loss. I am claiming the cost of repairs to my vehicle, £900, plus £75 for the cost of hiring a car while mine was off the road being repaired. Please find enclosed the receipted invoices from the garage and the car hire company.

Please pass this letter to your insurers. If I do not hear from you or your insurers within 21 days, I will start proceedings in the County Court to recover my losses.

Yours faithfully

Miss Susan Hammond

Figure 3. Letter before action to highway authority in a pothole claim

ZMA Insurance Ltd
Crown Building
UPMARKET

Miss S Hammond
5 Brook Street
UPMARKET
UP9 3SH

XX/XX/XX

Dear Miss Hammond

Re: Incident on B345 Upmarket road

We refer to your letter of the XX/XX/XX which has been passed to us by Upmarketshire County Council. Please note that we are the insurers of Upmarketshire County Council who are the highway authority for the area concerned.

We have received a full report from the highway inspector. In the light of its contents, we deny liability on behalf of the Council as we believe, in all the circumstances, they took reasonable steps to secure that the highway was not dangerous. Therefore, we rely on the statutory defence in section 58 of the Highways Act 1980.

We are sorry to hear of your misfortune but regret that we are not able to meet your claim as we do not believe our insured to be liable.

Yours sincerely

Figure 4. Letter denying liability on behalf of the Highway Authority

Road Traffic Accidents and the Uninsured Driver
So far in this chapter, we have assumed that the other driver is insured. Although by law a motorist is required to have insurance, unfortunately there are individuals who drive without it. What happens if you are involved in an accident with a motorist who is not insured? A person who is injured or has property damaged by an uninsured driver may be able to claim compensation from the Motor Insurers Bureau (MIB) – see Appendix D for the address. Also, a person injured by a ''hit and run'' driver may claim for personal injury but not for property damage. The MIB was set up in 1945 to establish a fund to compensate victims of uninsured drivers. All insurers are required to be members of the MIB. If you are involved in an accident with an uninsured driver, and the other driver was negligent, then contact the MIB who will send you a long form to complete. The MIB deals with the following situations:

- A claim for personal injury against an uninsured driver.
- A claim for property damage against an uninsured driver but not the first £175.
- A claim for personal injury against a ''hit and run'' driver.

From the information you give, the MIB will make enquiries and check that the other driver was uninsured. The MIB will usually appoint an insurance company to negotiate with you as though it were the insurance company of the defendant.

If settlement cannot be reached, the claimant is required to sue the driver in the normal way but must give notice to the MIB that court action is to be taken. If you obtain judgment against the uninsured driver and it remains unpaid after 7 days, then the MIB will pay the judgment provided you have transferred the judgment to the MIB. The reason you have to transfer the judgment is so that the MIB can recover money it has paid out from the uninsured driver. In the case of a claim for property damage, the MIB will not pay the first £175. Also, in the case of hit and run drivers, it will not pay property claims because of the risk of fraud.

Alternatives to Court Action

After you have sent the letter before action and 14 days have passed without a response or the reply you wanted, then you have to decide whether to take court action. It may be wise to pause and think, if you have not done so already, of the alternatives to starting a County Court action. Indeed, the recent civil procedure reforms encourage the claimant to consider the alternatives (such as mediation) before starting court action.

If the amount you are owed is £750 or more, sending a statutory demand to the defendant may force payment of the debt. As will be explained later, a statutory demand is the stage before you petition the court to make a debtor bankrupt (or insolvent if it is a company). The document demands that the debt be paid with 21 days otherwise you will press ahead with making the debtor bankrupt or insolvent. The threat of taking such action often produces payment.

If appropriate, you may wish to take advantage of any arbitration scheme provided by a trade association. All the alternatives to court action are considered in detail in Chapter 9.

The Financial Circumstances of Your Opponent

Apart from deciding the merits of your case, the most important thing to consider before going ahead with legal action is whether you are likely to receive any money from the defendant if you obtain judgment. It is not sensible to sue a person who clearly has no means to pay your claim. There may be satisfaction in obtaining judgment but you are effectively throwing money away. It may be that the defendant is ordered to pay by instalments – at such a low amount per week that it could take years to receive the total amount. In such circumstances it might even cost more to collect such small amounts than the debt itself. Many people are unaware that they have to enforce (collect) judgment. The actual process of applying to enforce judgment, for example an application for a "warrant of execution" which instructs the court to order a bailiff to seize the debtor's goods, will require the payment of a further court fee. That court fee is added to the amount of the judgment but that could be throwing more money away if you end up recovering nothing. (The various ways and procedures for enforcing judgment are explained in Chapter 8.)

Before issuing a claim, therefore, there are basic checks you should make into the background of the person you intend suing to see whether or not he is likely to pay after you obtain judgment. Check whether there are any judgments already registered against him. All County Court judgments for the past 6 years are listed in a central registry which anybody can search for a small fee. The register is maintained by Registry Trust Ltd (see Appendix D for the address). If there are several recent unpaid judgments against the person you are about to sue, there is a strong possibility that he will avoid paying you as well.

The Registry provides a form for a search but if this is not used then a letter, such as the example below, should be used instead.

Request for Search of County Courts Judgments Register

To: Registry Trust Ltd

Request for Postal Search of the Register

Please search the Register for the years xxxx to xxxx (inclusive) for entries against the following:

Surname:

Forenames:

Present Address:

Previous Addresses:

I enclose a fee of £ . . .

Signature:

Address:

Date:

In addition to searching the Register of County Court judgments, you could consider obtaining a financial status report. There are companies who will do this for a small fee and fax you within minutes a financial status report on a company which will enable you to make a speedy assessment of their creditworthiness. With modern technology and communications it has become easier to obtain information about people or companies at low cost. If you intend suing an individual or company for a reasonable amount of money it may be worth spending a few pounds to see if there is any likelihood of recovering the debt. Taking the trouble to obtain such information can avoid a lot of wasted time, effort and frustration.

4

STARTING COURT ACTION

- Introduction
- The Capacity in Which You are Suing
- The Defendant's Details
- Calculating the Size of the Claim and Interest
- The Particulars of Claim
- Which County Court Office?

Introduction

The previous chapter considered the steps to be taken before you start court action. If you receive no response from your letters, or negotiations fail, then court action is the next step. Going to court should be regarded as the last resort where all efforts to settle have failed. You should remember the ''no costs'' rule in the small claims court which means that you will only be able to recover the costs on the claim form. There are occasions when you may be awarded a small fixed amount, such as for expert or witness attendance. The matter of costs in the small claims court will be explained fully in Chapter 7.

In taking court action you have judged that there is a reasonable prospect of success. A reasonable prospect of success means that you have a better than 50:50 chance of succeeding. Points of principle and wanting your day in court are fine sentiments but you need to be realistic. Principles can end up costing more than you are ever likely to recover.

In starting a small claim it is important to prepare the claim carefully and describe clearly what it is you are claiming in the particulars of claim. Before sending the documents to court, you should consider these points as a check list:

- Are you suing the right person?
- Have you correctly described the defendant? (E.g. used the word "limited" if a limited company.)
- Is the address of the defendant correct?
- Do your particulars of claim clearly identify the basis of your claim and the remedy you are seeking from the defendant?
- Have you correctly calculated the size of your claim?
- Have you got the correct fee for the size of your claim?
- Do you have sufficient copies of the documents for the court office?

To start a claim you will need to take the following to the county court office:

- Completed claim form.
- Particulars of claim (if there is not room to state details on claim form).
- The appropriate court fee.
- Copies of the documents for service on the defendant.

You could ask the court to send the claim form in the post but you might wait a long time for it to arrive. It would be better if you collected it in person from your local court office. Also, be careful not to confuse the County Court with your local Magistrates Court, especially as many towns and cities have a building combining the two. The County Court deals with civil cases and is not concerned with criminal charges, which is the function of the Magistrates and Crown Court. The "claim form" is a court document which contains details of the claimant (the person making the claim), the defendant (the person being sued) and the amount and nature of the claim. The claim form should contain the following information:

● The full names and addresses of the claimant and the defendant.
● The remedy which the claimant seeks.
● Where it is a claim for money, a statement of value.
● Any matters which a court directive may set out.

The statement of value will either specify the amount of money you are claiming or state whether you expect to recover:

● Not more than £5,000.
● More than £5,000 but not more than £15,000.
● More than £15,000 or
● That you cannot say how much you expect to recover.

In a claim for personal injuries, you must also state whether the amount of compensation you reasonably expect to recover for the pain and suffering is either more or less than £1,000. It may be difficult for the lay person to know the likely amount of compensation for a personal injury. It would be sensible to seek advice in this respect.

In completing the claim form, you must ensure that you describe the parties in the correct way. The points you should consider are:

● The capacity in which you are suing.
● The legal status and the address of the person you are suing.

The Capacity in Which You Are Suing
It is important to consider in what capacity you are making the claim. If, for example, you are a sole trader doing business under another name, then you should use your own name

followed by the words "trading as". If you are a limited company bringing the claim, you must state "limited company" after the name then the trading address or the registered company office. Where you are a partnership, the words "a firm" should be used after the partnership name.

The Defendant's Details

It is crucial that you are suing the correct defendant and that you have their correct legal identity. There is no point in obtaining judgment only to discover later that you have wrongly identified the defendant. At this point it is worth checking the legal status of the defendant. If you believe you are suing a limited company that is registered in England and Wales, then contact Companies House in Cardiff. They can check the registered name of a company and its registered office. They will usually ask for the registered number of the company which should be on its stationery. They will instantly search the computer database to find the full company title and registered office. If you don't have a company registration number then give them the name you have and they will be able to discover whether it is a registered company and the address of the registered office. All of this can be done in a few minutes over the telephone and without charge. For the price of a telephone call you could save yourself a lot of problems later on. Where the defendant is a limited company, you should state the registered office or a place of business which has some real connection with the claim. If the defendant is a sole trader, you can sue them in their business name or their own name. However, it is best to state the defendant's own name followed by the words "trading as" and then the business name.

Where the defendant is a partnership, then you can either sue the partners under their partnership name or by naming individual partners. It is usually advantageous to sue a partnership using their partnership name because service is easier and proceedings simpler. (Further mention of this is made later on when the "service" of documents is explained.) After the name of the partnership, the words "a firm" or "sued as a firm" should be used. This indicates that the defendant you are suing is a partnership. How can you tell whether the organisation is a partnership? If it is a partnership the names of the partners are usually on their headed notepaper. If they are not, the names of the partners must be kept at the main place of business. The rules of the court provide that if you send a request in writing to the partnership then the names and addresses of the partners must be disclosed.

If the person you are suing is under the age of 18 the County Court regards him as a "minor". If a minor takes part in court action then he must do so through an adult. The adult is referred to as a "next friend" when the minor is the claimant and the "guardian ad litem" where the minor is being sued. The name of the next friend or guardian ad litem must be added to the title of the action. For example, if Brian Jones in Case Study 6 (Chapter 3) was a 17 year old driver the title would be as follows:

IN THE UPMARKET COUNTY COURT   CASE NO.

BETWEEN:

     FRANK SMITH   (Claimant)

     ----and------

     BRIAN JONES   (A minor by Fred Jones, his guardian ad litem) (Defendant)

Once you have correctly entered the names of the parties involved, you then have to give details of your claim. Enter a brief description of the type of claim, e.g. road traffic claim or sale of goods, and state "see attached particulars of claim". It is advisable to set out the details of your claim on a separate sheet of paper rather than trying to squash them into the claim form. By trying to cram details of your claim into this space you may omit important information. The only time it may be appropriate to enter details on the claim form is in a debt

action where you are claiming an unpaid invoice. Finally,
enter the amount you are claiming, the court fee (see Appendix C) and total it up in the box below. Do not enter anything
beside "solicitor's costs". You are only permitted to claim
solicitor's costs where a solicitor is acting for you and they
sign the claim form.

Calculating the Size of the Claim and Interest

You will notice that in the case study involving Frank Smith
and Brian Jones the amount being claimed for the damage to
the vehicle is £500. Frank is entitled to claim interest on this
under section 69 of the County Courts Act 1984 which
amounts to £6.14 (see below). Therefore the figure to be
entered on the claim form in the box marked "amount
claimed" is £506.14. In deciding whether the amount of the
claim comes within the £5,000 small claims limit, the court
disregards the court fees, any interest claimed under section 69
of the County Courts Act 1984 but not interest which is
claimed under the terms of a contract. Suppose your claim
amounts to £4,950. With the court fee and interest, the total
amount would be greater than £5,000. However, because court
costs and interest are disregarded the case would be within the
arbitration limit.

Interest may either be court interest or from a rate set in the
contract. In the road traffic case study, Frank claims £500 for
the cost of repairs plus interest from the date of the accident to
the date of the claim form at the rate of 8%; this amounts to
£6.14p. The interest rate of 8% is court interest, which Frank
is entitled to claim under section 69 of the County Courts Act
1984. If the claim was based on a breach of contract which had
a clause relating to interest, then that rate is used and it might
be more than the 8% set by the Court. The rate of court
interest you are entitled to claim under section 69 may vary
from time to time.

When calculating interest on a claim for a fixed amount you
need to show the following:

- The amount from the date the action arose or the debt became due to the date of the claim form.
- The daily rate at which interest will continue to accrue.

Calculating the Daily Rate of Interest
Example: £500 × 8% = £40 ÷ 365 days = 11 pence per day.

Therefore, to calculate the amount of interest from when the money became due to the date of the claim form, you simply multiply the daily rate by the number of days.

The reason for setting out the daily rate of interest is that, should he decide to pay the debt, the defendant is able to calculate the amount of interest due on any particular day after the date of the claim form. Obviously, where the amount being claimed is not fixed you will not set out the daily rate of interest in this way. When claiming interest on an amount that is not fixed, you need only state that you claim interest under section 69 of the County Court Act 1984 or the terms of the contract.

The Particulars of Claim
The particulars of claim set out the legal basis of your claim. It states all the relevant facts on which you rely and the remedy you are seeking. If particulars of claim are not contained in or served with the claim form, then it must be served on the defendant within 14 days after service of the claim form. The particulars of claim must include:

- A concise statement of the facts on which the claimant relies.
- The basis of the entitlement to interest.

Either the claim form or the particulars of claim must contain a statement signed by the claimant, or his legal representative, that the facts are true.

It is vital that you draft the particulars of your claim carefully. Make a plan listing the main facts of your claim in a logical order. Divide it into numbered paragraphs. As a general guide, the particulars of claim should include the following:

- Title of the action, i.e. who the action is between and the name of the court.
- Details of the relevant facts.
- The legal basis of your claim (e.g. the defendant's negligent driving).
- Signature and date.

The Particulars of Claim in a Road Traffic Claim

To get a better idea of the content and layout of the particulars of claim, study the sample particulars of claims appropriate for Frank Smith to use in his road traffic claim against Brian Jones. You will notice that Brian Jones is named as the defendant and not his insurance company. Many people make the mistake of naming the other driver's insurers as the defendant. However, it is the insurance company who is likely to pay any judgment. To ensure that you can make the insurers pay a properly obtained judgment against their driver, there is a procedure which you must follow at the time of issuing the claim or within seven days of doing so. You must serve notice in writing on the other driver's insurance company stating that you are starting legal action against their insured. This is a requirement under the Road Traffic Act 1988. If you forget to do this, the insurance company can avoid paying the judgment.

Particulars of Claim in Road Traffic Case Study

IN THE UPMARKET COUNTY COURT   CASE NO.

BETWEEN:

    FRANK SMITH   (Claimant)

    ----and----

    BRIAN JONES   (Defendant)

1. On the 5th June xxxx, the Claimant was driving a motor vehicle registration number...................., and the Defendant a motor vehicle registration number....................

The Claimant was stationary on the High Street at the junction with Baker Street waiting to turn right when the Defendant drove his vehicle into collision with the Claimant's vehicle as he attempted to turn right into the High Street from Baker Street. The collision caused damage to the front driver's side of the Claimant's vehicle.

2. The collision was caused by the negligent driving of the Defendant. As a result of the Defendant's negligence, the Claimant has suffered a loss.

3. PARTICULARS OF NEGLIGENCE:

— The Defendant cut the corner as he attempted to turn right.

— The Defendant failed to keep a proper look out and failed to notice the presence of the Claimant's vehicle on the road.

— The Defendant drove into collision with the Claimant's vehicle.

— The Defendant failed to avoid the collision with the Claimant's vehicle.

4. AND THE CLAIMANT CLAIMS:

1. The cost of repairs to his vehicle: £500.

2. Interest pursuant to section 69 of the County Courts Act 1984 at 8% being £6.14 from 5th June to the date of this claim and continuing at a daily rate of 11 pence until judgment or sooner payment.

Dated...................... Signed..

(Claimant)

The first paragraph identifies the claimant and defendant as driving motor vehicles. Quote the registration numbers of the vehicles involved just in case there is any dispute. It then sets out in sufficient detail what happened.

Paragraph 2 states the legal basis of the claim which is the negligent driving of the defendant. Mention should be made of the fact that a loss or damage was suffered as a result of the accident. It may sound obvious, but if the claimant has not suffered a loss, or an injury, then there is no claim to be made.

The next paragraph gives more details of the allegations of negligence. In many road traffic accidents, the issue of who was at fault is usually straightforward but there are some situations where it is not so clear. In the final paragraph, under the heading ''and the claimant claims'', state the sum of money or remedy being claimed.

In a road traffic claim, if the defendant has been convicted of a criminal offence arising from the accident, then include this in your particulars of claim. It is evidence of the defendant's negligence and makes your claim much easier because in some cases, such as convictions for careless driving or dangerous driving, it has the effect of reversing the burden of proof. If, for example, the defendant has been convicted of driving without due care and attention, this raises a presumption of negligence and it is for the defendant to disprove the presumption. Normally it is for the claimant to prove on the balance of probabilities that the defendant was negligent, but where the burden of proof is reversed, the defendant driver is assumed to have been negligent and it is for him to show that was not the case.

To take advantage of the fact that the defendant has been found guilty of a criminal offence arising from the road traffic accident, you must state in the particulars of claim:

● The conviction and date.
● The name of the court which made the conviction.
● The issue to which the conviction is relevant.

So if the defendant has been convicted of careless driving as a result of the accident he faces a difficult task to disprove negligence. To try and overcome it he may:

- deny the fact of the conviction,
- allege that the conviction was incorrect or
- deny that the conviction is relevant.

However, his task is not easy and so if the defendant driver has been convicted of careless driving then you are in a very strong position. Therefore, if you are aware that the police have investigated the accident you should find out if they are recommending prosecution for a driving offence. If the other driver is to be prosecuted, then you should wait for the outcome of the case. The police will not release their accident report until the criminal proceedings have been completed. If the driver is convicted, it is very unlikely that his insurers will contest matters when you write claiming your losses. Cases may take several months to be heard by the Magistrates Court but the verdict is vital to the question of liability in the civil action.

Not all road traffic convictions will have the effect of reversing the burden of proof, for example driving with defective brakes and drink driving, but they are very relevant to the issue of negligence. On their own, they are not evidence of negligence. In the case of drink driving, it could be argued that even if he was drunk, the accident was not caused by his negligence. Realistically, someone found guilty of drink driving is going to find it difficult to avoid a finding of negligence in a civil action because there is a presumption that he was unfit to drive.

Particulars of Claim in a Consumer Claim
Consider the sample particulars of claim which Judy could use in her claim against Upmarket Electricals regarding the faulty washing machine (Case Study 5, page 33). The particulars of claim includes all the important information. It describes:

- when the contract was made
- the subject matter of the contract
- the facts that gave rise to the claim

- the term in the contract which has been breached
- what the claimant claims.

It is important to have the date of the contract so that we know the claim is within the limitation period. The limitation period is the time period in which court action must be started. The limitation period for a contractual claim is 6 years. It is the same for a negligence action where there is no personal injury. Where the claim involves personal injury, the limitation period is 3 years.

The legal basis of Judy's claim is that there was a breach of an implied term of the contract because the goods were not of satisfactory quality. Paragraph 5 is included because if it is decided that the washing machine did not match the required quality but Judy had the goods for too long to reject them, then instead of awarding a full refund, the court can award compensation for the cost of repairs and other expenses.

Particulars of Claim in the Case Study Involving Judy and Upmarket Electricals

IN THE UPMARKET COUNTY COURT   CASE NO.

BETWEEN:

    MISS JUDY HOWE   (Claimant)

    ----and----

    UPMARKET ELECTRICALS LTD.   (Defendant)

PARTICULARS OF CLAIM

---

1. The Claimant purchased from the Defendant a new Hotspin washing machine for the sum of £500 on the 1st April XXXX.

2. Three weeks later, the washing machine began making a knocking noise and would not spin at the end of the wash cycle. The Claimant asked the Defendant to repair the washing machine but made it clear that by allowing the repairs she was not accepting the goods. The washing machine worked for a further 4 weeks and then it would not work at all.

3. The Claimant wrote to the Defendant on the 1st June XXXX stating that she was rejecting the washing machine on the grounds that it was not of satisfactory quality. The Claimant asked for the return of the purchase price but the Defendant has refused.

4. In selling goods that were not of satisfactory quality, the Defendant is in breach of an implied condition in the contract as to quality contrary to the Sale of Goods Act 1979, as amended by The Sale and Supply of Goods Act 1994.

5. The Claimant claims £500 being the purchase price, or in the alternative, damages for the cost of repairs and other losses as a result of the Defendant's breach of contract.

AND THE CLAIMANT CLAIMS

1. The said sum of £500.

2. Interest pursuant to section 69 of the County Courts Act 1984 being £10.01 from the date of the action to the date herein and continuing at a daily rate of £0.11 until judgment or sooner payment.

Dated..................... Signed...

(Claimant)

Particulars of Claim in Other Cases

● *Landlord and tenant disputes*

Tenants may experience difficulties in recovering deposits they paid at the start of the tenancy. If a tenant has fulfilled all his obligations under the tenancy agreement, then there should be no reason for the landlord to hold onto the deposit. If a landlord refuses to return a deposit at the end of a tenancy, then the tenant could make a claim to recover it. It would be a claim for a specified amount, i.e. the amount of the deposit. The small claims track also includes housing disrepair claims that have a financial value of not more than £1,000. This type of claim is where a landlord fails to comply with his obligation to maintain the property in a reasonable state of repair. This obligation may arise from the terms of the tenancy agreement or an Act of Parliament. An example of a disrepair claim would be where you discover that a window lets in the rain but the landlord fails to carry out repairs.

The particulars of claim in a dispute with a landlord over the return of a deposit need not be complicated. You should follow the basic principles considered when looking at consumer and road traffic claims. The information you should include is listed below.

- A brief description of the tenancy stating the date it terminated.
- Details of the deposit you paid and the basis on which it would be returned.
- That you fulfilled all your obligations as a tenant including the payment of all due rent.

Taking into account the above points, a particulars of claim for the return of a deposit from a landlord should be set out as follows:

PARTICULARS OF CLAIM

---

1. The Claimant was a tenant of the Defendant at 10 Market Street, Upmarket, from 1st January XXXX to the 1st July XXXX.

2. The Claimant signed the assured shorthold tenancy for a period of 6 months and paid one month's rent in advance plus a deposit of £350 which would be returned to the Claimant provided the Defendant had not suffered any loss or damage resulting from a breach of the tenant's obligations under the tenancy agreement.

3. On the 1st June, the Claimant gave one month's notice to terminate the tenancy as required under the tenancy agreement. On leaving the property on the 1st July, the Claimant had paid all rent that was due, had caused no damage to the property and had complied with all the obligations under the tenancy. The Claimant then requested the return of the said deposit of £350 but it has not been returned.

AND THE CLAIMANT CLAIMS

1. The return of the said deposit of £350.

2. Interest pursuant to section 69 of the County Courts Act 1984 being............. and continuing at a daily rate of............ until judgment or sooner payment.

(The sample particulars of claim refers to an "assured short-hold tenancy". This is a very common type of tenancy for short term lets but there are other types of tenancies.)

Which County Court Office?

The court rules allow you to begin your claim in any County Court in England or Wales. There are, however, a few considerations which might influence your choice of court. Where you are suing for a liquidated sum (i.e. a fixed amount, as in the case study with Frank Smith) then, if a defence is filed, the case is automatically transferred to the defendant's home County Court. (There is a proposal to stop this automatic transfer where the defendant is a company, but that would not stop a company from making an application to transfer.) If you object to the case being transferred to the defendant's home court then you must make an application to transfer the action elsewhere when you receive the new case number from the court to where it was moved. The district judge considers the application from the information submitted on paper and so you do not have to attend court. He may decide to transfer the case to a court which is convenient to both parties. However, it is still likely that the case will continue in the defendant's home court.

It is more convenient for you to bring your claim in your local County Court. It is much easier to be able to deliver documents in person to your local court office. So when completing the court claim form consider whether the defendant has an address in the area of your local court to avoid the automatic transfer rule. As was explained earlier, when suing a company the address you put on the claim form for service should be the registered company address or the address which has some real connection with the dispute. So suppose you bought a faulty television from the local branch of a major retail chain, the claim form can be served at the address from where you purchased the goods because it has a real connection with the dispute. If your claim is unliquidated, i.e. your claim is for damages and you cannot immediately say how much is being claimed, the automatic transfer rules do not apply.

When you take, or send, the completed claim and particulars of claim to the court office requesting that they be issued, ensure that you have sufficient copies. You will need a copy for each defendant. The original will be placed on the court file and a copy will be served on the defendant. It is best not to ask the court to make the copy which is sent to the defendant. It will charge over £1 per copy.

If you decide to take the completed claim form to the court office, the hours of opening are between 10am and 4pm Monday to Friday. The payment of the court fee can be made by cash or by a cheque supported by a cheque card, subject to it clearing and the Chief Clerk's consent. The court will accept solicitors' cheques. Most courts will accept payment by cheque, but if they are dishonoured then it will cancel the case for which the fee was paid. All cheques must be made payable to ''H.M. Paymaster General''.

5

SERVING THE CLAIM AND THE DEFENDANT'S REPLY

- Introduction
- Serving the Claim Form on the Defendant
- Responses from the Defendant
- Case Progression

Introduction

Having completed the claim form you need to send it (or take it in person) to the court, together with a copy and the appropriate fee. If you send it by post, it is advisable to enclose a stamped addressed reply envelope. The court will then check that the documents are completed correctly and will issue the claim form, i.e. formally stamp the claim form, give it a case number and provide you with a receipt for the court fee which is the Notice of Issue Form. The court will attach a Form of Reply which explains to the defendant how to respond and this must be served with the claim form. The court proceeding has now formally started and the claim form is ready to be served on the defendant. Service is where you notify the defendant of the claim form.

Serving the Claim Form on the Defendant

The court will serve the claim form by first class post unless the claimant wishes to serve it. The court is required to serve it as soon as possible. If the claimant wishes to serve it, the general rule is that it must be served within 4 months of being issued. The court rules provide that the claim form may be served in the following way:

- By the court by first class post except where other forms of service are permitted or requested.
- Service by the party may be by:

  i.   first class post
  ii.   personal service
  iii. fax machine
  iv. document exchange
  v.   leaving the document at a specified address
  vi. contractual service.

If a claim form is served by 1st class post, the date of service is the second day after posting. If you serve a claim form by leaving it at a specified address, the date of service will be the day after delivery. When served by fax, the claim form will be regarded as served on the same day if sent before 4pm on a business day. In any other case, service by fax will be on the following day.

It is usual to leave the serving of the claim form to the court unless there is some urgency. It may take 2 weeks for the court to issue and serve the claim form. However, it is advisable to let the court serve by post as there is less risk of there being a mistake in the service which could delay your case. The court will serve by ordinary first class post unless you request otherwise.

If the claim form is returned by the post office marked ''undelivered'' or ''not known'' then it has not been served. It is not unknown for debtors to return important looking documents marked ''gone away''. If the court sends out the documents by first class post and they are not returned, then they are presumed to have been correctly delivered and, therefore, served on the defendant. This presumption is rebuttable. Suppose the claim form is sent by post but does not arrive and is not returned to the court. The time for replying passes and the claimant applies for judgment in default. After having entered judgment in default, the court sends a copy to both parties. This time, the defendant receives the judgment in the post. He may apply to the court for an order to set aside the judgment on the grounds that he did not receive notice of the proceedings.

Where the claim form has been sent by post and returned to the court undelivered, a notice of non service is sent to the claimant.

A major problem when you are chasing people who owe you money is being able to trace their whereabouts so that you can serve the claim form on them. A common situation is where you let a property and the tenants leave owing rent or having caused damage to the property. Often the tenants disappear without giving a forwarding address and you are left with the problem of trying to locate them. However, you may be able to trace them by using an enquiry agent. There are a number of enquiry agents who specialise in tracing debtors who have absconded. Many enquiry agents are retired police-men who have useful contacts. They search credit reference databases and follow up on other sources of information to try and find the current address for the debtor. Many of these firms offer a 'no trace no fee' service. Obviously, the more information you have about the debtor – such as date of birth, national insurance number, any known family – the more likely it is that the enquiry agent will be able to trace them. It would be advisable to ensure that the enquiry agent you use operates within current legal requirements.

If you have made enquiries and are certain that the defend-ant is at a particular address but mail is merely being returned, then you could instruct the court bailiff to attend the defend-ant's address and personally serve the claim form by handing it to him or inserting it through the letterbox. If you do not know where the defendant is living but know his place of work, for example, then you could instruct an enquiry agent to personally serve the claim form by handing it to him in person. An enquiry agent will, of course, charge a fee. You may wish to personally serve the claim form but the enquiry agent is experienced at doing this job. If you decide to serve a document yourself, carry out the following procedure.

- Ensure it is the defendant by getting him to identify himself.
- Hand the claim form to him and if he refuses to take it, simply touch him with it and leave it at his feet.
- Swear a short affidavit to prove service has been effected and send a copy to the court. An affidavit can be sworn at the court office or before a solicitor who is a commissioner for oaths.

Many courts will send out a standard form of affidavit which you can use if you have to serve the claim form personally on the defendant. The court will also attach a copy of the forms for the defendant to reply to the claim.

The lay person may not understand what an "Affidavit" is, let alone know how to prepare one. An affidavit is a sworn statement which is used to support applications to the court or to give evidence. An affidavit is required to prove personal service of a document. It is useful to know the structure of an affidavit in case at some stage in your claim you are required to prepare one.

Sample Affidavit of Service

IN THE DOWNMARKET COUNTY COURT   CASE NO.

BETWEEN:

.... Claimant

and

.... Defendant

_____

AFFIDAVIT OF SERVICE
_____

I, Joe Smith, of 45 Downend, Downmarket, an engineer, make oath and say as follows:

1. I am the Claimant in the above action.

2. On the .... of XXXX I served the claim form on the defendant, a copy is attached and marked JS1, by delivering it personally to him at ....

Sworn at Downmarket County Court on the) ....

.... day of XXXX   ) Joe Smith

Before me ....

Fred Bloggs (Officer of the Court)

If you are required to prepare an affidavit for the court to support an application, the basic structure and wording should include:

● The names of the parties to the action and the case number.
● Begin with 'I, ..., of ...., make oath and say as follows:'.
● The main contents in number paragraphs.
● Always use the first person, i.e. 'I'.

Affidavits must be sworn before an authorised person. That could be a solicitor who is a commissioner for oaths or an officer of the court.

The Claim is Served

Case Study 8. Gary the electrician and the unpaid debt
Gary is a self employed electrician who did work for Boxed Houses Ltd at their new development in Upmarket. He sent an invoice to Boxed Houses for his wiring work at the site totalling £2,000. After sending two reminder letters the invoice remained unpaid and so Gary decided to issue court action. Gary lives in the County Court district of Downmarket. He attends Downmarket County Court and issues a claim form. The court serves the claim form on the defendant by

posting it first class on 4th May to the registered office of Boxed Houses Ltd which is in the district of Upmarket County Court.

The defendant has 14 days from the date of service in which to respond to the claim form. In the case of Gary and Boxed Houses, date of service will be on the second day after the 4th May. So if the claim form is posted on the 4th May, then the date of service is the 6th May. Boxed Houses have until the 20th May to respond to the claim form.

The court rules state that the claim form should be sent to the principal office of Boxed Houses Ltd or to any office of the company which has some real connection with the action. For the sake of certainty it is advisable to serve the claim form at the office registered with Companies House unless that office is not local to you and you want to avoid the case being transferred to another court. If the company states in corre- spondence that they would accept service at a particular office which is not the registered office, then serve the claim form at that address.

The defendant may respond to the claim form in one of the following ways.

- Pay the whole claim.
- Admit the claim and make an offer to pay.
- Admit part of the claim.
- Dispute the claim and enter a defence.
- Ignore the claim.

As was stated in Chapter 1, where the claim is below £5,000 the matter is automatically referred to the small claims proce- dure on the filing of a defence. The word "defence" includes when a defendant admits liability but disputes the amount owed. An example would be a defendant who admits respon- sibility for a road accident but denies that he caused the amount of damage which the claimant claims was caused to the vehicle.

The defendant must send an admission to the claimant

within 14 days of service. If the defendant enters a defence, he must send it to the court within 14 days of service – or within 28 days if a Notice of Intention to Defend has been filed. Suppose a claim form is posted on Tuesday the 2nd. It will not be deemed to have been served on the defendant until the 4th, so the defendant has in effect until the 18th to respond. If the claim is to be disputed by the defendant, provided he sends the statement before the 18th saying he will defend the claim, he has 28 days from the date of service (the 4th) in which to file his defence. The parties to a claim can agree, without the permission of the court, to extend the period for filing a defence by up to 28 days. The extension of the time will run from the date when the defence was originally due. If the parties agree to extend the time limit for filing a defence they must inform the court before the original period expires.

Responses From the Defendant
Defendant Admits Your Claim and Makes Offer to Pay
If the defendant admits your claim and offers to pay by instal-ments, what happens if you reject the offer? A court officer would decide what is a reasonable rate of payment and notify both parties. Either party then has 14 days in which he can apply for the rate of payment to be reconsidered by a district judge. However, be prepared for the court to decide a low rate of payment. Once the rate of payment has been set, a formal order is drawn up and sent to both parties. The defendant is warned that if he does not pay the instalments as ordered, then enforce-ment proceedings may be taken against him.

It is a well known frustration of creditors that debtors are ordered to pay a small amount per month. In some cases it takes many months or even years to pay off the debt. How-ever, if you believe the debtor's finances have improved, you can apply to the court to vary the rate of payment. If you wish to apply to the court, there is a standard form which should be used (N244). This is a general form and so can be used for other applications.

If you accept the admission and the offer to pay, you can then ask the court to enter judgment. To enter judgment, use the Notice of Issue form which contains a section for requesting judgment. If the defendant admits part of the claim, you cannot request judgment for the part they admit and pursue the balance.

The defendant, or his legal representative, may write a without prejudice letter offering to settle the claim on the condition that you withdraw court proceedings. It might also state that if you do not accept the offer to compromise then he will vigorously defend the claim. The defendant may be seeking time to pay without formally admitting the claim. If the defendant had returned the reply form admitting the claim but asking time to pay, you could enter judgment on the admission which the defendant wants to avoid. The defendant may be trying to protect his credit rating by avoiding a judgment being entered. If you agree to the defendant's offer to settle, then you should take steps to protect your position in case the defendant goes back on his promise. You would be advised to draw up a simple "Tomlin Order". This is a type of consent order named after the case in which it was first used. The effect is that the court proceedings are stayed (suspended) except to enable the parties to refer the matter back to court for the purpose of putting the agreed terms into effect. If you simply wrote to the court and asked for the action to be withdrawn and the defendant failed to do as promised, you could not restart the court proceedings. By drawing up a consent order with the correct wording, you could apply to the court to reopen proceedings and enforce the agreed terms. The wording of a consent order should be as follows:

IN THE .... COUNTY COURT   CASE NO.

BETWEEN:

.... (Claimant)

and

.... (Defendant)

CONSENT ORDER

Upon the parties having agreed terms of settlement

BY CONSENT

IT IS ORDERED

1. The Defendant shall . . .

2. All further proceedings be stayed save for the purpose of enforcing the said terms with liberty to apply for such purpose.

Dated ....

Signed ....

(Claimant)   (Defendant)

The Defendant Disputes Your Claim and Enters a Defence

If the defendant enters a defence, the court will send out an allocation questionnaire as was explained in Chapter 1. If the value of the claim is less than £5,000, the district judge will normally refer the case to the small claims procedure. The district judge may decide not to refer the case to the small claims procedure having considered the following:

- the financial value
- the nature of the remedy
- the likely complexity of facts, law or evidence
- the number of parties involved
- the value and complexity of any counterclaim
- the amount of oral evidence
- the importance of the claim to persons who are not parties to the proceedings
- the views expressed by the parties
- the circumstances of the parties.

If a defence is entered in a claim for a specified sum (fixed amount) and the defendant is an individual (not a company), the case will automatically be transferred to the defendant's home court.

After the case has been allocated to the small claims procedure, the district judge will:

- give standard directions and fix a date with a time estimate for the hearing
- give any special directions.

The district judge may direct that there should be a preliminary hearing and fix a date for that. He would consider whether or not such an appointment might help dispose of the case quickly where the claim is ill-founded or there is no reasonable defence. Although there is no requirement for district judges to do so, they tend as a matter of course to scrutinise defences in small claims to see if they are reasonable. The district judge may order that a full and proper defence be filed or the matter be struck out.

The district judge may give notice at the time of giving directions that he intends to deal with the claim without a hearing. In such a case, he would decide the claim on the documents filed by each party.

If no preliminary hearing is set, then standard directions are sent out and a hearing date is fixed with at least 21 days' notice to both parties. The parties can agree to a shorter period of notice. The standard directions with which both parties must comply are detailed below.

- At least 14 days before the hearing date, send the other party a copy of all documents you are going to use to prove your case.
- At least 14 days before the hearing date, send to the court and the other party any experts' reports you intend to rely on and a list of witnesses you intend to call.

A special direction may relate to the giving of expert evidence at the hearing. The allocation questionnaire requires each party to indicate if they intend to rely on expert evidence, either written or oral. So a special direction would state the permission required to use that expert evidence.

Where the defendant is a company, or the individual has a solicitor acting, it is not uncommon for him to contact the claimant for an extension of time in which to file the defence. Your first reaction will probably be to say no to such a request. It is common practice to allow one short extension of time if requested, for example 10 days. You do not have to agree to it. However, if the defendant was unable to file a defence in time and you entered judgment, he will probably make an application to set aside judgment. If there is a defence with a realistic prospect of success, the district judge will almost certainly set aside judgment and would regard your refusal to grant extra time as unreasonable conduct. In such a case, the judge might punish your unreasonable conduct by ordering you to pay the costs of the unnecessary application to set aside.

It takes on average about 3 months from the issuing of a claim form to the date of the arbitration hearing. The length of time it takes to receive a hearing date will vary depending on how busy the court is. If you can agree with the defendant to a shorter period of notice, then it might be possible to fix an earlier date for the hearing. If a particular County Court has many cases ready for hearing it is a matter of waiting for the next available slot in the court list. Where a district judge is a judge for two or more areas, he may at any time upon application – or upon his own motion – direct that the case shall take place in some other court of which he is a judge. This can reduce the delay in a case receiving a hearing date.

It could take longer than 3 months where you issue proceedings to recover a specified sum in a court which is not the defendant's home court. The case will automatically be transferred to the defendant's home court where the defendant is not a company. If the case has been transferred to a court which is a long distance away, you can apply to a district judge for the case to be heard at a more suitable venue. This application is made by putting your representations in writing to the district judge. The district judge decides the venue by considering the written submissions. However, it may take a while for the matter to go before a district judge. Before you can make an application to have it heard at a more suitable venue, you have to wait until you receive the new case number. Whether or not the automatic transfer causes a delay may depend on how busy the home court is. If, for example, you started your case in a relatively small court in a country town and the matter was automatically transferred to a busier court in a metropolitan area, then that is likely to cause a delay.

Where the opponent is a large company it is not unknown for a lawyer to be employed to delay proceedings for as long as possible. Such tactics are designed to make the ordinary litigant in person so frustrated that he decides not to pursue his claim. When a date for the arbitration hearing is set, each party is sent a Notice of Arbitration Hearing and this form states that if a party objects to it being dealt with under the small claims procedure, then an application should be made to the court. A defendant wishing to delay matters might decide to apply to the court to object to the case being dealt with by arbitration. The court will fix an appointment before the district judge to consider the objections.

Where the claim is for an unspecified sum, the case is not transferred automatically to the defendant's home court. However, if there is an application to set aside judgment in default, the case will be subject to automatic transfer (assuming the judgment was not entered in the defendant's home court).

These are the standard directions but each County Court may add its own directions, such as you must exchange copies of witness statements.

The Defendant Ignores the Claim Form

If the defendant does not reply to your claim form within 14 days, you can ask the court to enter 'judgment in default'. The court will check their file to ensure that no response was received from the defendant and then enter judgment.

However, this judgment may not be final. The defendant

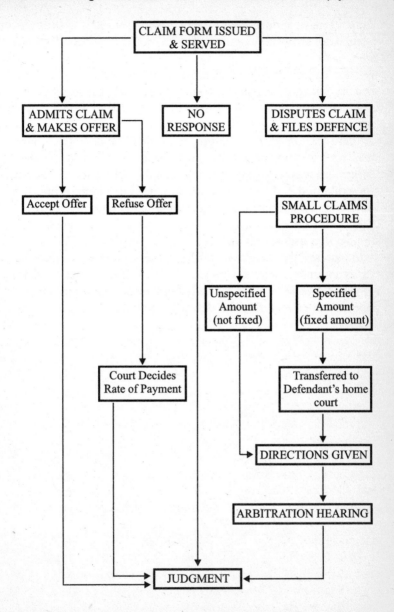

may make an application to the court to set aside judgment. A court may set aside judgment if:

- the defendant has a real prospect of success or
- it appears that there is some other good reason why the defendant should be allowed to defend the claim.

If there was an error in the procedure then the defendant may ask for the judgment to be set aside as of right. If the procedure was followed correctly then the defendant will have to explain the delay in responding to the claim form. In deciding an application to set aside judgment, the district judge will consider whether or not the defendant made the application as soon as was reasonably practicable. The court will not set the judgment aside if the defendant is merely delaying matters and has no real defence. If the district judge is uncertain, he may set the judgment aside on certain conditions, such as requiring the defendant to make a payment into court.

6

YOUR OPPONENT'S REPLY AND RESPONDING TO A DEFENCE

- Introduction
- Defences in Road Traffic Claims
- Defences in a Consumer Dispute
- Defences in a Highway Claim

Introduction

The previous chapter explained the serving of the court claim form and the possible responses from the defendant. This chapter examines an opponent's defence and how you should react to it. Also, the way to draft a concise defence is explained. You may think this is unnecessary if you are the person making the claim. However, having a good understanding of the likely defence is a good way to ensure you consider all aspects of your claim. Also, there will be occasions when you will be thinking of starting court proceedings but your opponent begins legal action before you. In these circumstances, you will need to know how to draft a defence and a counterclaim.

Only a few situations have been illustrated in this chapter but the following principles of preparing a defence are applicable to most cases. A defence must say:

- which allegation in the particulars of claim the defendant denies,

- which allegations he is unable to admit or deny but wishes the claimant to prove,
- which allegations he admits.

Where the defendant denies the claim he must state reasons for so doing and, if he intends to put forward his own version of events, state his own version.

If the defendant does not answer an allegation, then he might be deemed to admit it.

The previous chapter explained that if the defendant files a defence, then the matter is automatically referred to the small claims procedure provided it is within the small claims limit. It is possible, however, that the district judge may decide to call a preliminary hearing if he feels it may dispose of the case quickly and without the need for a hearing.

If the defence has no merit, the claimant can apply for summary judgment. Summary judgment is where judgment is entered without a hearing. The district judge will only enter summary judgment if there is no real defence and there is no other reason for a hearing to take place. The court rules provide that a district judge may order a party to clarify a matter which is in dispute in the proceedings and give additional information to such a matter.

Defences in Road Traffic Claims

Should you receive a court claim form in respect of a road accident, your insurance company will handle the defence of the claim. All you need do is send the court claim form to your insurers who will deal with the defence. It is unlikely that such a claim form would arrive unexpectedly. First, having been involved in an accident, you have a duty under your insurance policy to inform the insurer of the incident even if you do not make a claim. This will prevent you from being in breach of the contract with your insurance company. So they should have had notification of the accident. Secondly, you should have received a letter before action prior to any court proceedings which you would have also passed to your insurance company. From that point, they would have been in negotiation with the other party. When an insurer has been notified of a claim it will make investigations to decide whether or not the policyholder is liable. At this point, you will be asked to complete a report form. Therefore, if a claim form is received, the insurance company should already have details of the incident to enable them to prepare a defence.

Sample Defences in Road Traffic Claim

It is useful to consider what to expect if your opponent's insurance company enters a defence to your road traffic claim. An insurance company will most likely have instructed a firm of solicitors to draft the defence and it will be formal and technically worded. The case study involving Rebecca Cronje and Karl Smash is used to illustrate the layout and wording of a defence in a road traffic claim, together with the appropriate response.

Case Study 9. Road Traffic Accident: Rebecca Cronje and Karl Smash

Rebecca was driving along the B40, Upmarket to Downbridge Road, on a clear sunny morning. She approached the turn off for Downend and slowed down and indicated right before moving towards the middle of the road. She had noticed in her mirror, as she started to slow down, a red sports car approaching from behind. She looked forward and as there was no oncoming traffic, she started to turn right but her vehicle was struck by the red sports car driven by Karl Smash.

The facts of the case study involving Rebecca seem clear cut. She would argue that Karl Smash was negligent in that he attempted to overtake at a road junction. The Highway Code makes it clear that you should not overtake at a road junction as there is a greater risk of coming into contact with other road users. In this type of situation, it has been known that an opponent may try to argue a different version of events. Be aware that the defendant might say that you had moved over to the left of the road and started to slow down, creating the impression that you were pulling over and so he began to overtake. The important points in this case study are as follows:

- Did Rebecca indicate right?
- The position of her vehicle in the road just before turning right.

Rebecca decides to issue a claim form to recover the cost of repairs to her vehicle and hire car charges. An extract of her particulars of claim is shown below.

Rebecca's Particulars of Claim

PARTICULARS OF CLAIM

---

1. On the xx/xx/xx the Claimant was driving along the B40 Downbridge Road in her BMW reg. number .... and the Defendant a Ford Escort reg. number ....

2. The Claimant intended to turn right into Downend Road. As she approached the turn off, the Claimant slowed down, indicated right and moved towards the centre of the road. As the Claimant started to turn into Downend Road the Claimant's vehicle was struck on the front off side by the Defendant's vehicle.

3. The collision was caused by the negligent driving of the Defendant.

PARTICULARS OF NEGLIGENCE

— The Defendant overtook at a junction and when it was not safe to do so.

— The Defendant failed to take heed of the Claimant's presence on the road.

— The Defendant failed to keep a proper look out.

4. As a result of the Defendant's negligence, the Claimant has suffered loss and damage.

The basis of drafting a defence to a claim is that any issue raised in the claimant's claim should be denied otherwise it might be deemed to have been admitted. In the case study involving Rebecca, the insurers of Karl Smash instruct solicitors to enter a defence and counterclaim. It is likely to look something like that below.

Defence and Counterclaim of Karl Smash

DEFENCE

1. Paragraph 1 of the Claimant's claim is admitted.

2. Except to admit that there was a collision between the Claimant's and Defendant's vehicles, no admissions are made as to paragraph 2.

3. The Defendant denies that the collision was caused by his negligence.

4. Further, or in the alternative, the collision was caused wholly or in part by the negligence of the Claimant.

Particulars of the Claimant's negligence

— The Claimant failed to keep a proper look out.

— The Claimant failed to indicate.

— The Claimant turned across the path of the Defendant after pulling over and stopping at the near side of the road.

COUNTERCLAIM

5. The Defendant repeats paragraph 4 above.

6. As a result of the Claimant's negligence, the Defendant has suffered loss and damage.

The defence and counterclaim entered on behalf of Karl Smash argues that Rebecca pulled over to the near side of the road and, without indication, turned to the right. Whenever a counterclaim is entered with the defendant's defence, the claimant must serve a defence to the counterclaim otherwise it will be deemed to have been admitted. The claimant must serve a defence to the counterclaim within 14 days. It is not necessary to set out Rebecca's defence to the counterclaim as it merely denies the allegations that she was negligent. When a counterclaim is entered, a court fee is payable as if you were a claimant starting the action.

Defences in a Consumer Dispute

The case study involving Paul White and Auto Express Dealers concerns the purchase of a second hand car from a dealer. It is another example of when you need to enter a defence having expected to be the claimant.

Case Study 10. Paul and Auto Express Car Dealers

Paul White goes to Auto Express Car Dealers in Downend as he is interested in buying a second-hand sports car. Mr Jones, the Sales Manager, says that a 10 year old Dream Sports Car XRi will soon be coming into the showroom. Paul White states that it is important that he has the vehicle by the end of the month and that it must have electric windows because he cannot wind down windows manually because of arthritis in his wrist. Mr Jones says that he could sell the car to Paul for £3,000 but would require a deposit of £400, which Paul agrees to pay. The car is not delivered on time. A month late, Mr Jones receives the car and delivers it to Paul but he refuses to accept it because of the late delivery and he also notices that the car does not have electric windows as agreed. Mr Jones argues that there was a contract between the garage and Paul and would take the matter to court to enforce it. Paul replies by saying that any contract had been ended by the breach of the terms by Mr Jones because of the late delivery and the car not having electric windows. Paul asks for the return of the deposit but Mr Jones refuses.

Auto Express Dealers decide to take court action against Paul White. An extract of their claim is shown below.

Case Study 10. Particulars of Claim of Auto Express

1. The Claimant at all material times was a motor car dealer involved in selling cars in the course of its business.

2. On the XX/XX/XX, the Defendant attended the showroom in Downend and spoke to the Sales Manager, Mr Jones, about purchasing a second hand Dream Sports Car XRi. The Defendant was told by the Sales Manager that there would be one coming into the showroom.

3. The Defendant made an offer to purchase the said vehicle for £3,000 which the Claimant accepted and the Defendant paid a deposit of £400. The balance of £2,600 to be paid on delivery.

4. In breach of the contract to purchase the motor car, the Defendant refused to accept the vehicle when the Claimant delivered it.

5. As a result of the Defendant's breach of contract, the Claimant has suffered a loss.

AND THE CLAIMANT CLAIMS:

— Damages for breach of contract.

The basis of Auto Express Dealer's claim is for non-acceptance of goods where they comply with the contract and the consumer refuses to pay for them. In a sale of goods contract, this is governed by section 50 of the Sale of Goods Act 1979. A consumer who wrongfully fails to accept goods or services may first of all lose any prepayment he has made, which is usually the deposit. Also, the supplier may claim damages for the consumer's breach. The measure of damages is the loss directly and naturally resulting from the alleged breach of contract. Where there is an available market for the goods, this would be the difference between the contract price and the market price when the goods ought to have been accepted.

The basis of Paul's defence is that the contract with Auto Express Dealers was at an end because of their breach of two fundamental terms. The two main terms that were breached were:

- Time was "of the essence" and the vehicle was delivered late.
- The vehicle did not have electric windows.

A statement that time is "of the essence" means that that term is vital to the contract and so late delivery will discharge the contract. Paul could question whether in fact Auto Express Dealers have actually suffered a loss. There is a duty on Auto Express to mitigate their loss. This means that the garage have to take reasonable steps to reduce any loss. So they should put it back out in the showroom in an attempt to sell it to another customer. If they do sell the vehicle relatively quickly, the market price may not have fallen much and taking into account the deposit, the garage may not have suffered a loss.

On the facts of the case (assuming his version to be accurate) Paul appears to have a good defence and a strong counterclaim for recovering his deposit.

Paul's Defence and Counterclaim to the Claim by Auto Express Dealers

DEFENCE

1. It is admitted that the Defendant attended the Claimant's garage to purchase a Dream Sports Car XRi motor car.

2. The Defendant stated that he must have delivery of the vehicle by the end of the month and that time was of the essence. Also, a term of the contract was that the vehicle must have electric windows. The Claimant said that he would be able to deliver the car by the required time and it would have electric windows. The Defendant therefore offered to buy the vehicle for £3,000, which the Claimant accepted, and paid a deposit of £400.

3. In breach of the terms of the contract, the Claimant was late in delivering the vehicle and it did not have electric windows. As a result of the fundamental breach of the contract, the Defendant was entitled to treat the contract as discharged and therefore refused to accept the vehicle.

4. In the circumstances, it is therefore denied that the Claimant is entitled to damages.

COUNTERCLAIM

5. The Defendant repeats paragraphs 1 to 4.

6. As a result of the Claimant's breach of contract, the Defendant has suffered a loss.

AND THE DEFENDANT COUNTERCLAIMS:

— The return of the deposit of £400.

It is important to set out a defence and counterclaim in numbered paragraphs. Instead of repeating the information in the defence for the counterclaim, you can simply refer to the relevant paragraphs in the defence.

Defending a Claim for a Dishonoured Cheque

Many people attempt to resolve consumer problems with self-help remedies such as cancelling a cheque quickly when they discover a problem. If you purchase goods and services with a cheque but later cancel it before it is presented to your bank, the trader has an action against you for dishonouring a cheque under The Bills of Exchange Act 1882. Stopping a cheque is an understandable reaction when you have bought faulty goods or have received poor service. The problem is that if an action is brought for dishonouring a cheque, it may be difficult to argue that you have received nothing at all from the contract, especially where services are concerned. The case study involving David Parker and the Castle Hotel examines what defence you may have if you are faced with a claim for a dishonoured cheque.

Case Study 11. David Parker and the Castle Hotel

David Parker organised a Christmas party for his 30 work colleagues in the accounts department. He decided to book the banquet room at the local Castle Hotel in Downend. The hotel has a reputation for good food and a high standard of service. However on this occasion, the food was under-cooked, cold and in small portions. Also, the service was very slow and the waitresses were rude because the party took a while to decide which wine they would have with the meal. David Parker was presented with a bill at the end of the evening for £600. After making his dissatisfaction perfectly clear to the manager, he reluctantly paid the bill with a cheque. After talking with colleagues the following day, he decides to stop the cheque. He receives a letter from the restaurant owner demanding payment. David Parker is adamant that he is not going to pay anything for what he regarded as an awful meal. The restaurant owner says he will take him to court.

When faced with a claim for a dishonoured cheque, a defence you have would be to argue that there has been a "total failure of consideration". This means that you got no value/benefit from the contract, i.e. the meal was so terrible that David Parker and his party gained no satisfaction from it and so should not pay anything. It is unlikely that a judge would accept this argument. The meal may have been awful but they did have a meal, albeit an unpleasant one, and so they did receive something in return. A judge is likely to say that a reasonable price for the meal was less than £600 and so award the restaurant owner a much lower amount.

If Mr Parker was going to cancel his original cheque then it would have been advisable to have sent another one, stating that it was in full and final payment of the bill because he considered that to be a reasonable price in the circumstances. The restaurant owner may then have thought twice about going to court because there is a risk that the lesser amount is all he may be awarded. It is probable that in such a situation the restaurant owner may simply put the matter down to experience and take no further action.

If the Castle Hotel decide to take court action against Mr Parker for stopping the cheque, the claim would be worded as set out below:

Extract from a Claim for a Dishonoured Cheque

1. The Defendant drew a cheque for £600 dated the XX/XX/XX upon Upmarket Bank payable to the Claimant.

2. The Claimant duly presented the said cheque for payment on the XX/XX/XX but it was dishonoured because payment had been countermanded by the Defendant.

3. The Claimant claims interest under section 57(1) of the Bills of Exchange Act 1882.

AND THE CLAIMANT CLAIMS:

    i. The said sum of £600.
   ii. Interest pursuant to section 57(1) of the said Act.

It has been stated that the defence to a claim for a dishonoured cheque is that there has been a "total failure of consideration". An appropriate defence to the claim by Castle Hotel would be:

1. The Defendant drew the said cheque in favour of the Claimant in consideration for the Claimant providing food and service at the Claimant's restaurant at the Castle Hotel.

2. It is admitted that on the XX/XX/XX the Defendant cancelled the payment of the said cheque. The food and service provided by the Claimant's restaurant was so poor that there was therefore no consideration for the said cheque.

3. It is therefore denied that the Claimant is entitled to the relief that is claimed or any relief.

The sample defence could also set out the details of why there was no consideration (or nothing in return) for the cheque. In this case, Mr Parker should set out the details of the terrible meal at the Castle Hotel. It is unlikely that Mr Parker will get away with paying nothing. Therefore, an alternative is for Mr Parker to admit that he cancelled the cheque but dispute the hotel's entitlement to claim the full £600. It would then be for the Court to decide what was a reasonable price for the meal he received.

Defences in a Highway Claim

Chapter 3 contained Case Study 7 of Susan and the damage to her vehicle from driving through a pothole. It was stated that Susan's claim is based on section 41 of the Highways Act 1980. The highway authority is under a duty to maintain the road in a reasonable state of repair. Susan has to show that the highway was not reasonably safe and that the dangerous condition of the road caused the accident. The highway authority may argue that the defect in the road did not constitute a hazard, but frequently it will attempt to establish the statutory defence under section 58 of the Highways Act 1980.

It would be useful to examine in more detail the nature of this defence under section 58. Anybody who drives regularly in the UK will know that many of the roads are in a poor state of repair, due to more cars and restricted maintenance budgets. This has led to a big increase in claims for damage caused to vehicles from potholes and more people seem to be claiming for injuries caused by tripping over uneven pavements. Some of the increase in highway claims has arisen from the greater tendency to sue. Therefore, the defence under section 58 has become increasingly important in the highway authority's attempt to defend the growing number of cases.

Section 58(1) of the Highways Act 1980 states:

"In an action against a highway authority in respect of damage resulting from their failure to maintain a highway maintainable at the public expense it is a defence . . . to prove that the authority had taken such care as in all the circumstances was reasonably required to secure that the part of the highway to which the action relates was not dangerous for traffic."

Section 58(2) sets out a number of matters which the court must consider when deciding whether or not the highway authority has established this defence. These matters are:

- The character of the highway and the traffic expected to use it.
- The standard of maintenance appropriate for a highway of that character and used by such traffic.

- Whether the highway authority knew, or could reasonably have been expected to know, that the condition of the highway was likely to cause danger.
- Where the highway authority could not reasonably have been expected to repair the highway, what warning notices were displayed.

In the case study involving Susan, the insurers for Upmarketshire indicated in their correspondence (see Figure 4 in Chapter 3) that they would be relying on section 58 to defend the claim. If Susan issues a claim form to recover the cost of repairs to her vehicle, she is likely to receive a defence that would contain a reference to section 58. An extract of the likely defence to be filed by Upmarketshire County Council is shown below.

Extract from the Defence in the Highway Claim

DEFENCE

3. It is denied that the Defendant was in breach of its duty to repair or maintain the said highway. At all material times it took reasonable care to secure that the said highway was not dangerous for traffic, and the Defendant relies upon section 58 of the Highways Act 1980.

4. The said highway is inspected every 4 months with the last inspection having taken place 2 months prior to the Claimant's alleged accident when the highway was found to be safe.

It is useful to understand the basis of the defence that could be raised by the highway authority. It will assist you in preparing your case if you know the likely arguments they will use.

When a defence has been entered by the defendant, is there a need to enter a reply to the defence? Lawyers will give you differing answers to this question. It is usually not necessary to enter a reply to a defence unless there is clearly some new issue which has been raised and you wish to respond. Generally, a reply to a defence is not necessary in a small claim.

7

THE COURT HEARING

- Introduction
- Preparing Your Case for the Hearing
- Documents and Witnesses
- The Day of the Hearing
- Costs and the Right of Appeal

Introduction

The hearing of a small claim is informal. It takes place in the district judge's chambers in private. The parties sit around a table. The judge does not wear a wig or gown, which adds to the informality. The strict rules of evidence do not apply and the district judge has the power to conduct the hearing as he feels is appropriate. He will probably ask that any oral evidence is given under oath. If a party is not represented at the hearing the district judge will assist by asking the witnesses appropriate questions. In fact, the judge will take a fairly active role. Even if a party is represented, it is unlikely that the advocate will be permitted to make lengthy contributions. After all, the idea of the small claims procedure is to avoid the need for lawyers.

We saw in the previous chapter that, prior to the court hearing, each party has to conform with the directions laid down by the court. These directions are the timetable which the case follows. In a small claim, each party must exchange,

14 days before the hearing, a copy of any document on which they intend to rely in court and a copy of any expert's report must be filed at the court. Although there is no rule requiring a copy of any factual witness statement to be exchanged some County Courts have their own local directions to this effect. If this direction is not complied with the statements/documents may not be allowed as evidence at the hearing.

Preparing Your Case for the Hearing
To illustrate how to prepare and present your case, consider the case study involving Julie and the purchase of a second hand car.

Case Study 12. Julie and the second hand car
Julie sees an advert in the local newspaper.

"Ford Escort 1600. Tidy bodywork and good runner. £2,950 o.n.o. Tel 01248 123243". Julie went to the seller's house with her friend, Brian, to view the car. Julie asked Mr Shifty about the phrase "good runner" because it was important that the car was reliable. What was the mechanical history during his ownership? How many times had it broken down in the last 10,000 miles or so? Mr Shifty replied "It has not broken down recently". On hearing that she decided to make an offer of £2,800 which he accepted.

Three days and 50 miles later, Julie was driving to work when the car came to a halt. Fortunately she is in the AA and calls out a patrol. The patrolman spotted that the clutch had worn out completely. Also, he noticed one of the cylinders was not working which he suspected from the uneven idle. This was confirmed by connecting it up to a tuning instrument. Julie was towed to her local garage. The mechanic, John Franks, said to Julie that by chance Mr Shifty had recently had the car serviced at his garage. He had told him that the clutch was worn right down and may fail shortly, plus the fact that the engine was running unevenly when he took it for a test drive. However, Mr Shifty told the mechanic to adjust the play on the clutch as far as he could to make it easier to change gear. He said he was about to sell it. Julie is told by the garage that it will cost £175 plus labour to replace the clutch and £300 plus labour for the work on the cylinders. She is given an estimate for the total work of £775. Julie is obviously disappointed because she feels that Mr Shifty misrepresented the mechanical condition of the car. Had she known the condition of the vehicle, she would not have bought it.

Julie writes to Mr Shifty and asks for the contract to be set aside and her money back. Mr Shifty denies that he misrepresented the condition of the car. Julie attends a free legal surgery at her local solicitors to discuss whether she has grounds for a claim.

The basis of Julie's argument is that there was a misrepresentation by Mr Shifty. It was explained in Chapter 2 that a misrepresentation is an untrue statement of fact that induces the party to enter into the contract. The Sale of Goods Act does not apply to private sales and so Julie cannot argue that the car was not of satisfactory quality.

The advertisement described the car as a ''good runner'' but this could be classed as mere sales talk which is not specific. However, the vital part of the claim is the response to Julie's question which she asked to clarify the meaning of ''good runner''. She wanted a car that was reliable and so asked direct questions about the car's mechanical history. Julie asked whether the car had ''broken down'' in the past 10,000 miles and he replied that it had not ''broken down recently''. The evidence from the garage mechanic (see above) seems to suggest that this was untrue or a half truth. According to an old case of *Dimmock v. Hallett (1866)* stating only half the facts which gives a misleading picture can amount to a misrepresentation.

The vital aspects of Julie's case will be:

- The evidence of her friend Brian.
- The evidence of the garage mechanic.
- A report by the AA patrolman as to the mechanical condition of the vehicle.

Brian will be able to give evidence as to the specific questions Julie asked Mr Shifty when she went to view the car. Brian's evidence also backs up Julie's claim that the mechanical condition of the car was important and so Mr Shifty's statement induced her to buy the vehicle. The garage mechanic's evidence will be used to argue that Mr Shifty's statement that the vehicle had not broken down recently was untrue. It also suggests that Mr Shifty was aware of the worn clutch. The mechanic, John Franks, states that it was running unevenly and cut out when he took it for a test drive. The AA patrol man may not be needed to give oral evidence at the hearing but it would assist to have a written report that would provide evidence of what was the cause of the breakdown.

A good way to prepare your case is to anticipate the arguments of your opponent. Mr Shifty is likely to say that the response to Julie's question was true. In strict terms, this may be correct. The car may have been running unevenly for some time and the clutch was very worn but it could still be driven and so had not "broken down recently". However, a car that was running unevenly and had a very worn clutch is unlikely to have been a smooth "runner".

The evidence suggests that Julie has a reasonable case. If she prepares her case carefully and the evidence comes across well, then she has a good chance of winning.

Documents and Witnesses

To decide which documents you need to exchange and the witnesses to call, list the points you need to make to prove your case and support each one with a document or the evidence of a witness. In the case of Julie, this would be as follows:

- The statement(s) made by Mr Shifty: *the evidence of Brian plus the advertisement.*
- This statement was untrue: *the AA report and John Franks the mechanic.*
- The statement induced the contract: *the evidence of Brian.*

So the documents on which Julie will want to rely at the
hearing will be the newspaper advertisement and the report of
the AA patrolman. It would also be advisable to exchange
copies of statements detailing the oral evidence to be given by
Julie's friend Brian and the garage mechanic John Frank. You
will remember from Chapter 1 that on the filing of a defence
the court sends out an allocation questionnaire. This questionnaire contains a section relating to expert witnesses. In this
part you will need to state if you intend to submit the report of
an expert. Julie would have stated that she intended to use the
AA report. In the small claims procedure, neither party may
use expert evidence – whether written or oral – without the
district judge's permission. This permission is given in the
directions that are sent out following the allocation of the
claim to the small claims procedure.

Statement of Brian Turner

I, Brian Turner, of 20 Church Gardens, Upmarket, will say as
follows:

*1. On the 20th March XXXX, I was asked by Julie Marshall if
I would go and look at a car with her which she had seen
advertised in the local newspaper. She said she was looking to
buy a reliable car. She told me she was interested in a Ford
Escort 1600, XXXX model, which was described as being a
"good runner" and having tidy bodywork.*

*2. We arrived at the defendant's house and saw the Ford
Escort parked in the driveway. The bodywork was indeed tidy.
The engine was started but because it was cold it required a
lot of choke. Mr Shifty did not allow Julie or me to take the
car for a test drive. Julie then asked Mr Shifty about the
mechanical history of the vehicle. Julie told Mr Shifty that it
was important that the car was reliable. She then asked him
how many times had the car broken down in the previous
10,000 miles or so. Mr Shifty replied, "It had not broken
down recently". On hearing this, Julie made an offer of
£2,800 which was accepted.*

The contents of this statement are true to the best of my knowledge and belief.

Signed....................................... Dated.......................................

The statement from Brian Turner will be the basis of his oral evidence. The statement should be in the witness's own words. Set out the statement in numbered paragraphs. Ensure that the statement is signed and dated. You will be given 21 days' notice of the court hearing which will give you time to inform your witnesses and allow them to take time off work to attend. You may find that witnesses change their mind about attending and giving evidence as the hearing approaches. It is possible to obtain a witness order which will mean the witness must attend. However, a reluctant witness is worse than no witness. You would be best advised to present your case in the best way possible without that witness.

Statement of John Franks

I, John Franks, of Upmarket Garage, will say as follows:

1. I am a mechanic at the Upmarket Garage. I have 10 years' experience as a mechanic.

2. On the 10th March XXXX, Mr Shifty brought his Ford Escort in for a service. He asked me to do a basic service, which is a change of oil and new points and plugs. After doing the service, I took the car for a test drive. I noticed that the clutch was very worn and that the engine was running unevenly making it cut out on a few occasions. I told Mr Shifty about the worn clutch and that it may fail soon. I also asked if he wanted me to investigate the uneven running of the engine. He told me to adjust the clutch as far as I could to make the gear change easier but nothing else as he was selling the car soon. This I did and he collected his car on the 12th March.

Witnesses may be daunted at the prospect of giving evidence in court. Reassure them that the hearing of a small claim is an informal occasion in the private room of the district judge.

There are no wigs or gowns; just both parties to the dispute sat around a table. The public or press are not allowed in. This may remove any worries the witness may have about what to expect. It is advisable to meet with your witnesses before the hearing to go over their evidence. Let them refresh their memory from the statement you took. However, do not coach the witness as to what they will say.

Extract from the report prepared by the AA Patrol

CONCLUSION

On examining the car, I found that the clutch was worn. Also, I noticed that the engine was running unevenly at idle. On further inspection, I found that one cylinder was not working and that it was badly worn.

A witness might be worried he will become flustered if questioned by a razor sharp barrister. Explain to him that it is unlikely that the other party will be legally represented, and if he is, it will almost certainly not be a top flight barrister. Legal representation is not encouraged at a small claims arbitration because the system is designed for the lay person to bring his claim himself. Though you can have legal representation, this is less likely because of the no cost rule, which means that you cannot be awarded your legal costs of the arbitration.

Alternatively, you may wish to have a lay representative to speak on your behalf at a small claims hearing. (Lay representatives are given this right under the Lay Representatives (Rights of Audience) Order 1992.) This would allow you to have an advice worker from the Citizens Advice Bureau to speak on your behalf or other types of lay representatives, some of whom provide such services commercially. Unless you feel so overcome by nerves that you will not be able to explain your case, there is no great advantage in having representation at a small claims hearing. The district judge usually takes an active role in the proceedings. Therefore, if you know that you will not recover your legal costs it does not make sense to have a lawyer present to make a very minor contribution. Also, the issues are usually straightforward. If the case was more complicated then the judge would have transferred the case out of the small claims procedure.

The Day of the Hearing

When you arrive at the court, check in at the desk with the court usher. He will mark on the case list that you are present. Sit in the waiting area and you will be called when your case is called. Be prepared for a long wait. Courts are well known for running over their schedule times. It may be that in the waiting area the defendant comes over and makes an offer to settle the case. If this happens, still go in before the district judge and state that the matter has been settled. In this situation, it would be wise to set out the terms that you have agreed in a written document. Both parties can then sign it and send a copy to the court office for it to be stamped and placed on the court file. Lawyers call such a document a "consent order". It is useful to do this because if your opponent goes back on the offer to settle, you have a legally enforceable agreement. Such a document should always include a clause that if the defendant fails to do as promised, the court case may be restored.

When your case is called, the court usher will show you into the district judge's chambers. As the claimant you normally sit on the right hand side of the table as you look at the judge. The district judge should be addressed as sir or madam. He (or she) will then make a note of each party and any representatives that are present.

The district judge will have already read the papers on the court file. It is therefore important that you clearly expressed your case in the particulars of claim when you started proceedings, so that the judge will already have a good understanding of the issues.

The procedure followed at the hearing will vary depending

on the district judge. The County Court Rules[1] permit the
district judge to adopt any method of procedure he may
consider fair. Unless the judge orders otherwise, oral evidence
need not be given on oath. However, experience suggests that
oral evidence is usually given on oath. Where both parties
appear without representation, the case is likely to be conducted in the following way:

- The district judge may indicate what he considers to be
  the issues, explaining any relevant matters of law.
- Each party will then be questioned about his case and
  asked about points raised by his opponent or any witnesses.
- The district judge may take the evidence as a whole from
  either side or, in more complicated cases, he may deal
  with each issue separately.

When the judge asks you to put your case you should have
prepared a concise opening statement which outlines your
claim and states what you are seeking from the defendant.
Avoid rambling on about irrelevant matters or exchanging
insults with your opponent. If the defendant becomes disrup-
tive, perhaps interrupting, compose yourself and don't retali-
ate. It may work to your advantage. If you stay calm and stick
to the evidence, then any bad behaviour by the defendant may
mean that the district judge forms a bad impression of your
opponent.

It will help your presentation if you prepare an indexed
bundle of the documents to be used at the hearing. Provide
copies for the judge and your opponent. You will immediately
find favour with the judge if he can easily find the documents
you refer to in your case.

The opening statement with which Julie could begin might
be as follows:

_____

[1] County Court Rules, Order 19, rule 9

... "Sir, my claim is that the defendant misrepresented the mechanical condition of the car. I will present evidence to show that his statement that the car had not broken down recently and that it was a good runner was untrue. I relied on the truth of Mr Shifty's statement and decided to buy the vehicle. A few days later the car broke down and it required £775 of repairs. I am claiming that the contract should be set aside and that the defendant refunds the purchase price of £2,800 ..."

This opening statement is not legalistic. You are not a lawyer and so will not be expected to present your case like a lawyer. Speak slowly and clearly, with one eye on the judge who may be making long hand notes. Above all, avoid the temptation to make an impassioned plea like a lawyer in a television drama. The judge is interested in the strength of your evidence and not your oratory.

After making your opening statement, go through your claim referring the judge to the documents you are relying upon. The case involving Julie will depend more on the oral evidence of her witnesses. Other types of cases, such as debt actions for unpaid goods or services, are likely to depend more on documentation. Often in these cases, documents will be relied upon to show what the terms of the contract were and that the debt is due. In the case of a road traffic claim, the documents you might rely on (and so need to exchange) could include:

- Photographs of the scene of the accident.
- A police report (if they attended).
- Garage estimates and receipts showing the cost of the damage to your vehicle.
- Receipts for hire cars when your vehicle was off the road.

The case study involving John Stopflow concerns a debt action. John's claim is for the balance of an invoice which relates to work he carried out for Fred Brown.

Case Study 13. John Stopflow and the bathroom suite

John Stopflow is a plumber who specialises in fitting new bathrooms. He was contacted by Fred Brown and asked to provide a quote for installing a new bath/shower unit. John took measurements of the bathroom and provided Fred with a selection of designs to choose from. He provided Fred with a quote detailing the overall cost of the job including the labour and a list of the fittings to be installed. Fred accepts John's quote of £2,000 and asks him to do the work. John completes the work and submits an invoice for payment within 14 days. The invoice states that Fred Brown should contact John if he is not satisfied with some element of the work. Payment is not received and he sends a follow up letter. Two weeks later he receives a cheque for £1,000 with a note saying that the shower does not work properly and the bath is the wrong size.

If John takes Fred to court for the remaining amount, he would want to rely on the quote to show the terms of the contract to supply and fit the bath/shower unit. In presenting his case, John would emphasize the point in the invoice that Fred should contact him if he is dissatisfied with the work. It was only after sending a chasing letter that Fred made contact. On the point of the bath not being the right size, John should state that he had provided various designs and it was Fred who selected that particular unit.

In addition to preparing an opening statement, it is useful to have thought of some questions you want to ask the defendant. Questions should focus on areas where you want to challenge the defendant's case. A good way to question a defendant, especially where you doubt the accuracy of his evidence, is to ask him to explain in more detail a particular matter. The hope is that he may trip himself up by saying something which is inconsistent with his earlier evidence. In the case involving John Stopflow, he should ask Fred Brown why he had not complained earlier if the shower was faulty. You may think of questions to ask when you receive any documents which the defendant is going to use at the hearing. However, do not worry if you are uncertain about what to ask your opponent.

The district judge will usually assist both parties by asking appropriate questions to draw out relevant information.

Costs and the Right of Appeal
Costs in the Small Claims Procedure
As already stated, there is a ''no costs'' rule in the small claims procedure. This means that no solicitors' charges or the costs of a ''litigant in person'' (a person without representation) are to be recovered from the losing party except:

- Court costs stated on the claim form.
- The costs of enforcing the award, e.g. the cost of requesting the court bailiff to execute a warrant.
- Other costs which the district judge decides when there has been unreasonable behaviour on either side in relation to the proceedings of the claim.

The district judge has discretion to award costs in certain other situations for certain allowances. He can award a sum for the report and attendance of an expert witness. In addition, a small amount can be claimed for witnesses (which includes the party to the case). The winning party may be awarded a small amount towards travel expenses. An amount may be awarded to the successful party for legal advice he has obtained to bring or defend a claim for an injunction or specific performance. An injunction is where you are asking the court to order that a person be stopped from doing a particular act. Specific performance is when you ask the court to order another person to fulfil obligations under a contract. However, as the judge has discretion it means that he has the power to make these awards but may not do so. In deciding whether to award anything for the cost of an expert's report, the judge might consider whether it was in fact necessary.

Generally, only the court fees on the claim form and the costs of enforcement can be claimed. If you need to take enforcement measures to collect your money from the defendant, you can add these costs to the amount of the judgment. So if you decided to apply for a Warrant of Execution, the court fee that is required is added to the total amount you want the bailiff to try and recover.

The district judge has the power to award costs if there has been unreasonable conduct by a party to the claim. The recent case of *Chohan v. Newbold (1997)* is an example of when a district judge may award costs for unreasonable conduct in small claims. The case concerned a road traffic accident. The defendant accepted that the claimant was established on a roundabout at the time of his entry and that he struck the claimant's vehicle in the middle with the front of his vehicle and that he had skidded upon braking to avoid the collision. Two days before the hearing the defendant made an offer of 50 per cent of the sum claimed. The claimant rejected the offer. The claimant succeeded in his claim and applied for costs. The judge said that needless litigation should be discouraged. Where the defendant continues to proceed when he has a hopeless case, holding out to the last moment could be regarded as unreasonable conduct. The defendant ought to have put in a realistic offer to avoid the award of costs. Both parties in this case were funded by insurers and the judge made a distinction between this situation and where parties were privately funded.

Appealing Against the Decision
The right of appeal from a small claims hearing is very limited. The appeal can be made only on the grounds that:

- there was a serious irregularity affecting the procedure or judgment, or
- the judge made an error of law.

A party may only appeal if the court gives permission. To seek permission, you must apply to the court that gave judgment and set out your grounds. You must make this application within 14 days after the notice of the judgment has been served.

Non Attendance at the Hearing

It is common for defendants not to attend the hearing in debt actions; the defendant will often file a defence to a claim but have no intention of attending the hearing to argue his case. It is a tactic to gain extra time to pay, or perhaps, time in which to disappear. If a party is not going to attend the hearing then he should give notice to the court at least 7 days before, stating the reasons why he will not be attending. The court may then take into account that party's statement of claim and any other documents he has filed when it decides the case. If a claimant does not attend the hearing and does not give notice, the court may strike out the claim.

8

ENFORCING JUDGMENT

- Introduction
- Oral Examination
- The Methods of Enforcement and their Effectiveness
- Selecting the Appropriate Method of Enforcement
- Being Realistic About What You Will Recover
- The Lord Chancellor's Review of Enforcement Procedures

Introduction

Once you have obtained judgment it is up to you to enforce (collect) payment. The court does not do this automatically. You have to apply to the court with the appropriate fee. There are various methods of enforcing judgment. In some cases, such as a road traffic claim where the defendant is insured, receiving payment is unlikely to require enforcement measures. Provided you have observed the correct notice procedures, a road traffic insurer is obliged to settle any judgment entered against their insured.[1]

---

[1] Except in certain circumstances where the policy was obtained by non-disclosure or misrepresentation of a material fact and the insurer obtains a declaration of the court to that effect.

All money judgments of over £1 are registered at The Registry of County Court Judgments in London. If the whole amount is paid within one month, the entry can be removed. To remove the registration of a judgment you must produce proof to the court that entered the judgment that it has been paid. The court will then issue a certificate of cancellation for a small fee. If payment is made after one month, you can apply to have the entry marked as satisfied but the record will remain on the register for 6 years.

Therefore, it is advisable for the debtor to pay in full rather than by instalments if he has the money available. This fact can be used to persuade the debtor to pay in full within a month. Receiving payment in full is obviously better than having to wait many months, even years, for the debtor to settle the judgment by instalments.

Having a County Court judgment registered against your name makes it very difficult to obtain credit. Banks, credit companies and other lending institutions will obtain a credit report before making a decision whether to lend money. This will include a search to see if there are any registered County Court judgments. If there are, it is unlikely that they will grant a loan. This is one reason why it is not advisable to ignore a County Court claim form.

Many people are not aware that it is for them to decide whether (and how) to enforce a judgment, not the court. There are several methods of enforcing a judgment and how to apply for each will be explained later in this chapter. The methods of enforcing a judgment are:

- A Warrant of Execution
- Attachment of Earnings
- Garnishee Order
- Charging Order.

Oral Examination
Before examining the methods of enforcement, it is sensible to think about ways to find out about the defendant's means. This could be done by:

- instructing an enquiry agent to find out financial information about the defendant or
- applying to the court for an Oral Examination.

The problem with enquiry agents is that they can be expensive. If you are claiming a small amount then it will not be economic to instruct them. The Oral Examination has the benefit of requiring answers to be given on oath.

An Oral Examination is used to find out the financial means of the defendant. The defendant is required to attend at court and answer questions on oath about his financial circumstances. The plaintiff is required to send a request for an Oral Examination to the Court where judgment was entered, together with the court fee.

The court will then fix a date and the defendant will be ordered to attend. The form of request is shown in Appendix A. It is served on the defendant by post as if it were a claim form. A financial means questionnaire is enclosed with the notice of the Oral Examination. This gives the defendant the opportunity to submit information in advance of the hearing and make an offer of payment.

If the defendant fails to attend an Oral Examination, the court sets another date. It is served on the defendant with a committal notice which warns that failure to attend again could mean the debtor being committed to prison for contempt of court.

At the Oral Examination, an officer of the court will ask the debtor a series of set questions. You are also allowed to ask the defendant questions. The following are the type of questions:

— *What assets do you own?*
— *Are you owed money? If so, by whom?*
— *Do you have a job? If so, where? What is your pay?*
— *Do you have a bank account? If so, where and what is the account number?*
— *Do you own your own house? If you own your own house,*

how much is it worth? How much is owed on the mortgage?

An Oral Examination provides valuable information about the defendant to help you decide the appropriate method of collecting payment. In the case study involving Graham Holder (see below), it is apparent that he does have means to pay the judgment. In some situations, a debtor may not be so open about his financial situation if he is trying to avoid paying. However, the court does have the power to commit the debtor to prison for contempt if he refuses to answer questions. An Oral Examination is probably most effective as a weapon to warn the debtor that you are serious about collecting payment. If debtors fail to attend the hearing it is served again with the threat of a committal order. This often produces a response.

At this stage the debtor will often put forward a payment plan. If you accept the offer of payment, then the court will draw up an order to that effect. The order will state the date when the first payment must be paid and will warn the defendant that if payment is not received, then other enforcement action may be taken by the claimant. If you reject the offer of payment, then an officer of the court will decide the amount the defendant should pay, taking into account his financial situation. This can sometimes be a small amount of money each month, which means that it could take a long time for the debt to be paid. If, subsequently, you have reason to believe that the debtor's financial circumstances have improved, you can make an application to the court for the order to be varied. So, for example, if you are aware that the debtor has just obtained a well paid job when previously he was unemployed, it is worth applying to the court to order the debtor to pay increased instalments.

The next case study involving Graham Holder and Red Brick Supplies concerns the non-payment of an invoice for the supply of building materials. It will demonstrate why it is worth finding out the financial circumstances of the defendant before starting enforcement proceedings.

Case Study 14. Red Brick Supplies and Graham Holder

Red Brick Building Supplies Ltd sold materials to Graham Holder, a self employed builder, for a total sum of £1,500. These materials were required by Holder so that he could commence work on the extension he had been contracted to build at a house in Upmarket. Red Brick were quite happy to let Holder have the materials on credit as he had been a regular customer and had always paid invoices on time. Red Brick supplied the usual invoice allowing 30 days to make payment. However, on this occasion the account was still unpaid after some 45 days. Red Brick then sent two letters chasing payment before issuing a County Court claim form. Holder entered a defence claiming that the materials were substandard and refused to pay. The matter went to a hearing at which the district judge gave judgment in favour of Red Brick. Red Brick now have the task of enforcing judgment to recover the £1,500.

The answers given at the Oral Examination in this case study are set out below. It provides some valuable information.

Oral Examination of Graham Holder

Do you have a bank account?	Yes
With which bank?	Upmarket Bank Plc
What is the account number?	00245654
Is this account in credit? If yes state the amount.	£4,000
Do you own any assets?	Yes. I own a Range Rover worth £10,000.
Do you own your own property?	Yes.
How much is it worth?	£55,000 approx.
Is there a mortgage on it?	Yes £50,000

Based on these answers, Red Brick Supplies could choose
between a Warrant of Execution, a Garnishee Order or securing the debt by obtaining a Charging Order on Graham
Holder's property. An Attachment of Earnings order is not an
option because Graham Holder is self employed; the debtor
must be an employee.

The Methods of Enforcement and their Effectiveness

Having obtained financial information about the defendant
from the Oral Examination, or through an enquiry agent, you
will need to decide how to enforce the judgment. Let's look at
how you apply for the various methods of enforcement and
consider the effectiveness of each method.

A Warrant of Execution

A Warrant of Execution is the most common form of enforcement. It is a request for the court bailiff to seize personal
belongings of the debtor. The personal belongings are sold and
the proceeds of the sale, after costs, will be paid to the
claimant up to the value of the judgment.

To issue a Warrant of Execution, you need to send to the
court:

- A copy of your judgment.
- A completed form N323 (a Request for a Warrant; see
  Appendix A).
- The appropriate court fee.

You should apply to the court where the judgment was
entered. If the debtor has moved to another district, the court
will send the Warrant to the bailiff in the area where the
defendant lives.

A completed request for a Warrant in respect of the case
study *Red Brick Supplies v. Graham Holder* is illustrated in
Appendix A (page 142).

A Warrant of Execution may be the most common form of
enforcement but it may not be the most effective. It will only

be effective if you know the debtor has assets of value and can direct the bailiff to them by providing the addresses. The bailiffs will only act on information provided and will not carry out their own investigations. Debtors who are deliberately avoiding payment may move items to unknown addresses to prevent the bailiffs seizing them. The fact that some bailiffs send a 7 day letter before executing the warrant also gives the debtor the opportunity to move items of value.

Bailiffs do not have powers to force entry to premises. There are proposals being considered that include granting bailiffs powers of entry but there are objections on the grounds of civil liberties. It is, therefore, unlikely that such proposals will be implemented. Often, when the bailiff arrives to execute a Warrant, he will be met with claims that the property on the premises is not owned by the debtor or is on hire purchase. Also, the debtor may at this last minute put in an application to suspend the Warrant and be given further time to pay the judgment. In these circumstances, if the claimant does not grant the debtor time to pay, or permit payment by instalments, it will be up to the court to decide whether or not the debtor's offer is reasonable. In reaching a decision the court will take into account the financial circumstances of the debtor. These last minute applications buy time for the debtor. In the meanwhile, some debtors will undoubtedly take the opportunity to disappear. You are then faced with further time and expense in tracking them down.

Despite the potential problems with requesting a Warrant of Execution it can be effective if used in the right circumstances. In some situations, and depending on the person you are pursuing, having the bailiffs knocking on the debtor's door may produce the required result. It will show the debtor that you do not intend to let them avoid payment. Hopefully, you will receive a reasonable offer. The effectiveness of a Warrant of Execution depends on the court bailiff. Experience suggests that some court bailiffs are more effective than others.

Attachment of Earnings Order

This occurs when the court orders the defendant's employer to make deductions from his earnings and pay them direct to the creditor. The order can attach to wages, commissions and bonuses. The amount of the judgment must be more than £50. Deductions cannot be made from social security benefits or retirement pensions. If the defendant is a serviceman, then you must approach The Defence Council (see Appendix D) who have the power to make deductions from servicemen's pay. In other cases, the way to apply for an Attachment of Earnings order is as follows:

● An application on form N337 (see Appendix A) which certifies the balances due.
● The appropriate court fee.

If the defendant has moved into the area of another County Court, then you must first write to the court where the judgment was entered and ask that the case be transferred to the County Court where the defendant now lives. On receipt of the transfer, the court will give the case a new number. Also, if you are applying to a court other than where the judgment was made, you will need to send a copy of the judgment.

The application is then served on the defendant and they have 8 days in which to complete and return a form detailing their financial circumstances. If the debtor does not reply in time the court asks the employer to give details of the debtor's earnings. The employer must provide a statement of earnings otherwise the court can impose financial penalties.

When the court has received details of the debtor's earnings, it will decide an appropriate amount to be deducted. The court will then issue a provisional order and if you object to the amount then there will be a hearing before the district judge.

An Attachment of Earnings order is only of use if the debtor is in regular employment. Each time the debtor changes employment, you have to make another application. The advantage, however, is that the payments will be made on a regular basis.

Garnishee Order

Where the debtor is owed money by another party or someone holds money on behalf of the debtor, you can apply for a Garnishee Order so that the money be paid directly to you to settle your judgment. A common example of when you might apply for a Garnishee Order is when the debtor has a bank account which you know is in credit. Another example is where the debtor is owed money by another person. You could apply for a Garnishee Order so that the third party is ordered to pay the money direct to you.

To apply for a Garnishee Order you need to send to the court the following:

- An Affidavit in Support on form N349 (see Appendix A).
- The appropriate court fee.

The application is made ''ex parte'' which means that the defendant is not given notice. The obvious reason for this is that if the defendant was given notice then he may remove funds from the bank account. The court considers the application and if granted draws up an ''Order Nisi'' which orders the third party to hold any money until there is a hearing at the court to establish if the money should be paid to you. This Order Nisi is served on the person holding the money (''the Garnishee'') at least 15 days before the hearing and then on the debtor 7 days later.

As can be seen from the Affidavit in Support (form N349), you have to state the reason why you believe the Garnishee is indebted to the debtor. You may state that your belief is based on an Oral Examination or that the Garnishee has confirmed this information.

The Garnishee Order operates at the precise moment it is served. So if the order was served on the defendant's bank but there was no money in the account, then the application would fail. If the debtor has written a cheque out on that account the day before the order and is in the clearing system, that cheque will be paid because it has a prior call. Where the account is in joint names, the Garnishee Order will fail unless both account holders are the judgment debtors.

A Garnishee Order is a useful method of enforcement because it can be effectively used to freeze the debtor's bank account. However, the court will not permit such an application to be used as a "fishing expedition". You have to convince the court that you know of the existence of an account held on behalf of the debtor. Also, it is often the case that the account is not in credit.

Charging Orders
A Charging Order is a way of securing the debt on the debtor's property or shares they have in a company. It does not in itself provide you with actual payment of the debt but the defendant cannot sell the property without your being paid. Once you have a Charging Order, you can then apply to the court to force sale of the property and so receive your money.

The starting point is to find out if the debtor owns property. If you know where the debtor lives you can search the Land Registry to discover whether or not he owns the land. This will only be possible if the land is registered. Properties that have not been bought and sold for a long time may be unregistered. It is not possible to do a search for the owner of shares in companies.

To apply for a Charging Order, you need to prepare an Affidavit (see Chapter 5) which contains:

- The name and address of the debtor and any known creditors.
- The amount outstanding on the judgment.
- The identity of the property to be charged.
- The reason for your belief that the debtor owns the property, i.e. refer to the land registry title.

The Affidavit is then sent to the court with the appropriate fee. The application is made "ex parte" which means that notice is not given to the defendant. The court considers the application and, if satisfied, makes a Charging Order Nisi. This Order Nisi is the first step toward obtaining a full Charging Order. The Order Nisi contains a date for a hearing at which the court considers whether the Order Nisi should be made absolute. You, not the court, must serve a copy of the Order Nisi on the defendant at least 7 days before the date of the hearing.

It is advisable to collect a copy of the Order Nisi straight-away so that it can be registered at the Land Charges Register (if the land is unregistered) or at the Land Registry (if the land is registered). The Land Registry is divided into regions and you will need to ensure you send it to the correct office. There may also be a fee that is payable and so it would be advisable to contact the appropriate office to find out how much it is. Once the Order Nisi is registered at the Land Registry (or Land Charges Registry), a "caution" will be marked against the property. This will protect your interests pending the hearing. If you do not, the defendant may mortgage the property and that would take priority ahead of any Charging Order that is granted.

At the hearing to decide whether or not the Order Nisi is made absolute, the defendant has the opportunity to say why the court should not grant the Charging Order. The district judge has discretion whether or not to grant the Charging Order. This means that he is not bound to grant the Charging Order. District judges have been known not to grant a Charging Order because the amount of the judgment is very small.

Charging Orders followed by an application for sale of the property can be an effective method of enforcing your judgment. However, this assumes that when the property is sold there are sufficient funds available to pay off your debt. It may be that there are many creditors ahead of you who have already obtained a charge over the property so that if it were to be sold, there would not be enough money left over to pay you. Also, experience suggests that courts are more reluctant to grant an order for sale. The judge will often adjourn an application for sale of the property to allow the judgment debtor a chance to make proposals to clear the debt.

Selecting the Appropriate Method of Enforcement

The case study involving Upmarket Housing Association concerns a former tenant who left owing rent of £90.

Case Study 15. Upmarket Housing Association

Helen was a tenant of Upmarket Housing Association. Helen's rent was £45 per week for a small studio flat. She was not working and so her rent was paid by Housing Benefit. The Housing Association was not permitted to take a deposit from Helen when the tenancy began. She left the property owing £90 in rent arrears. The Housing Association takes her to court and obtains judgment, which, including costs, amounts to £100.

What would be the best method of recovering £90 in rent? Suppose you discover that Helen is now working. Would you apply for an Attachment of Earnings order? It would probably be most appropriate to request a Warrant of Execution. Using a bailiff is more effective when the amount is relatively small. It is likely that Helen would have something worth seizing to settle a debt of £100. When the debt is larger, there is less chance of there being enough goods to seize. Also, the cost of requesting a warrant in this case is less than the fee for an Attachment of Earnings Order. The procedure for an Attachment of Earnings order is likely to take longer than the issue of a Warrant of Execution. Experience suggests that where the amount is small defendants sometimes believe that you will not bother to pursue it and so wait until the last moment. By instructing the bailiffs, the debtor will know you will not let the matter drop.

Earlier, the procedure for requesting an Oral Examination of a judgment debtor was illustrated by the case of Graham Holder and Red Brick Supplies. It was explained that the option of an Attachment of Earnings order is not available because Graham Holder is self employed. Which of the remaining enforcement options is most appropriate? Assuming that Graham Holder does not make an offer to pay on receiving the order to attend the Oral Examination, a Garnishee Order would seem appropriate. The answers to the Oral Examination show that his bank account is £4,000 in credit. If Red Brick decided on this option, they should act swiftly before Graham Holder removes money from the account.

It would seem from the Oral Examination that Graham Holder does have the financial means to settle the debt. He owns assets well in excess of the £1,500 judgment and so instructing the bailiffs should be considered. He owns a property but there is a mortgage on it. He states that there is a mortgage of £50,000 on it, which would mean there would be sufficient funds if the property was sold for £55,000. However, the property market can fluctuate and so the value of the property could fall and, taking account of sale costs, there may be a situation of negative equity. This means that the value of the property is less than the mortgage and other charges secured on the property. If Red Brick are seeking to recover their money quickly then a Charging Order followed by an application to force sale may not be the quickest method of enforcement.

In all the circumstances, Red Brick would be advised to apply for a Garnishee Order.

Transferring to the High Court to Enforce
If the debt is less than £1,000, then it has to be enforced through the County Court[2]. However, if the debt is above £1,000, you have the choice of enforcing it in the High Court or County Court. The relevance to a small claim would be where you were seeking to recover between £1,000 and £5,000. If you wanted to enforce your judgment in the High

---

[2] The High Court & County Court Jurisdiction (Amendment) Order 1997

Court, you first have to transfer the matter to the High Court. There are some advantages of enforcing your judgment in the High Court: you will be able to claim interest on the judgment; and there is evidence to suggest that the High Court Sheriff, who is the equivalent of the County Court Bailiff, takes a more robust approach to enforcing a Warrant.

Being Realistic About What You Will Recover

It is important to be realistic about what you will recover from the defendant and how long it will take. A report by The Consumers' Association (November 1997) suggests that many people using the small claims court regard the enforcement procedures as slow and inefficient. The report found that only a minority of defendants had paid on time, and after six months a large minority had still not paid.

There are various reasons which might explain the large number of unpaid judgments. Many people are still unaware that the court does not enforce judgments but that it is the responsibility of the winning party. Even if they know they have to enforce their judgment, they may not have a good knowledge of the various procedures. Another factor is certainly the gradual rise in the small claims limit over the years. This caused an increase in small claims and perhaps a large portion of these cases were started without considering the financial means of the defendant. Often, because of the 'no-costs rule', claimants feel that it is worth taking a chance as they only stand to lose the court fee. Of course, some people are not too concerned at recovering their money because they brought the claim as a matter of principle.

The Lord Chancellor's Review of the Enforcement Procedures

The Lord Chancellor's department is looking at proposals to improve the enforcement procedures. In Spring 1998, the Lord Chancellor announced a review of the methods of enforcement. It is not expected to produce a report until Summer 2000. The review is to look at ways to improve the effectiveness of current enforcement procedures. As well as considering ways to improve current methods, it is willing to examine possible new methods. If the review leads to any changes, they are not expected to be implemented until Autumn 2001.

Along with looking at the current enforcement methods, which have been discussed in this chapter, the review will consider whether or not:

- New methods of enforcement might be introduced.
- New types of sanctions could be applied when debtors fail to comply with court orders.
- There need to be changes to the court's role in the enforcement process, e.g. granting greater powers to court bailiffs such as a right of entry.

In launching the review, the Government consultation paper "Enforcement of Civil Court Judgments" (June 1998) acknowledged that increasing the efficiency and effectiveness of the available enforcement methods is not the whole answer. Many creditors find their choice of enforcement restricted by the circumstances of the debtor. This means that even if the present system was made more efficient, there would still be cases where recovering money is going to be difficult, if not impossible. This country is unlikely to return to sending debtors to prison and without such a threat to bad payers things may not improve very much. It is likely that, at the end of the review, the basic methods of enforcement will remain, with perhaps modifications and maybe some new procedures. Even if changes are suggested, such as greater bailiff powers, it will probably be a long time before they are implemented, if at all, because of the civil liberty implications.

9

ALTERNATIVES TO COURT ACTION

- Introduction
- Ombudsmen
- Trade Associations
- Mediation
- Statutory Demands
- The Media

Introduction

In Chapter 3, a brief mention was made of the alternatives to court action. This chapter examines in more detail some other ways of trying to resolve your dispute. Experienced lawyers can give the impression that if your opponent does not settle then the only option is to launch into court action. The lay person could be forgiven for thinking that this attitude regards any other action as a sign of weakness. In recent years, especially since the review undertaken by Lord Woolf, lawyers are being trained and re-educated on alternatives to court action. One of the themes of the Woolf Report is the view that court action should be regarded as the last resort. Cynics may argue that this attitude has been developed because the civil justice system cannot cope with the large increase in cases. Also, some might suspect that Governments are not prepared to fund the legal system to the extent that is required to manage the greater number of civil cases. However, claimants want to achieve a fair result within a reasonable time scale. If they achieve this without the need for court action, then that is a benefit.

This chapter examines the role of trade associations, ombudsmen's schemes and mediation as means of resolving a dispute without court action. In addition, the threat of a statutory demand will be explained as a way of forcing payment from a reluctant debtor.

Ombudsmen

Many service industries belong to ombudsman schemes which enable disputes with their consumers to be resolved relatively simply. An ombudsman is an independent official appointed to investigate complaints by individuals, or companies, of unfairness or maladministration. The motorist is likely to be aware of the Insurance Ombudsman who investigates complaints against insurance companies. The Insurance Ombudsman can investigate companies if:

- The insurance company is a member of the Ombudsman Bureau.
- A senior manager in the insurance company has made his final decision.
- The complaint concerns you personally.
- The policy was issued in the UK.
- It is about a claim or the administration of your policy.

The Insurance Ombudsman will not investigate if:

- Legal proceedings have started.
- Your dispute is with another person's insurance company.
- Your complaint is about the level of premiums or decisions as to the level of cover.

One of the largest number of complaints concerning motor insurance relates to the replacement value paid out after the car has been written-off or stolen, and this figure has been increasing. There are now about 300 complaints a year. The case study involving Richard and Cheap Insurance Ltd is a typical example of a dispute over the valuation of a vehicle.

Case Study 16. Richard and Cheap Insurance Ltd
Richard had an accident in his ten year old Ford Escort XR3i. The vehicle is badly damaged and his insurers, Cheap Insurance Ltd, declare the vehicle a write-off. Richard has comprehensive insurance and waits to be paid the replacement value of the vehicle. Cheap Insurance offer Richard £1,500. Richard is not happy with the valuation as he feels the car was worth about £2,500 because it was in excellent condition.

How should Richard try and persuade Cheap Insurance to increase their offer? Before negotiating with his insurance company, he should understand what he is entitled to receive for the written-off car. He is entitled to the market value of the Ford Escort prior to the accident. In the Ombudsman's report of 1995, the market value was described as being the cost to replace the vehicle with one of a similar age, condition, mileage and so on. It is not the private market which might be seen in local newspapers. The policyholder is entitled to receive what it would cost to replace the vehicle through a motor dealer. Insurance companies for many years based the replacement value on the private market until the guidance provided by this report.

Richard is entitled to the market value of the Ford Escort prior to the accident. In deciding the replacement value, all relevant evidence should be considered. The Ombudsman favours the use of trade guides. Richard may be able to negotiate an improved offer from Cheap Insurance by sending evidence to support the value as being £2,500. Insurance companies often make a low first offer. To increase their offer, Richard sends the following to Cheap Insurance:

- A note of the relevant pages in trade guides, such as Parker's or Glass's Used Car Guide.
- Copies of the service history of the vehicle to show that it was kept in excellent condition.

- Details of the mileage.
- A letter from a reputable local dealer giving their opinion of what it would cost to purchase a Ford Escort of that age, condition, mileage etc.

On receipt of the documents to support Richard's valuation, Cheap Insurance may increase their offer. If the offer is greatly improved so that it is close to what Richard wants, then he would be advised to accept it. So if Cheap Insurance offered £2,300 after seeing the evidence supplied by Richard, it would be sensible to accept it. Suppose, for example, their second offer was only increased to £1,600. This is still a long way from the £2,500 he believes it is worth. In this case, it would be worth taking the matter further.

Richard's options are to take Cheap Insurance Ltd to the small claims court for a breach of contract or ask the Insurance Ombudsman to adjudicate on the fairness of the offer. If Richard asks the Ombudsman to investigate, he can still take the matter to court if he disagrees with the valuation. Before asking the Ombudsman to investigate, Richard should write one further letter similar to the one shown in Figure 5.

The Insurance Ombudsman will decide if it is a complaint the Bureau can investigate. If the complaint is investigated, they will request to see the insurance company's file. If the Ombudsman adjudicates in favour of Richard, then Cheap Insurance Ltd are bound by the decision. This means that if they wish to remain a member of the Ombudsman scheme, they will have to comply with the award.

The Insurance Ombudsman Bureau is independent of the insurance companies. Figures from a recent year show that of the 311 cases relating to motor car valuations, 32% were decided in favour of the policyholder, i.e. the person bringing the complaint. This may seem a large number decided in favour of the insurance company, but perhaps policyholders are not realistic about the values of their vehicles.

Another area of common complaint concerns repairs carried out by a garage nominated by the insurance company. These

25 Market Square
UPMARKET

The Claims Manager
Cheap Insurance Ltd
Insurance House
UPMARKET

XX/XX/XX

Dear Sirs

**Re: Replacement Value – Ford Escort 1.6 XR3i
reg. F666EBA**

Policy Number: 000333444555666777RB

I refer to my letter of XX/XX/XX in which I enclosed
evidence to support the view that the market value of the Ford
Escort was £2,500.

I note that the offer in your previous letter was £1,600, less
the policy excess of £100. I feel that this is considerably lower
than the vehicle was worth and hope that you will reconsider.
Would you please confirm whether or not this is your final
offer. If it is, then I intend to apply to the Insurance
Ombudsman to adjudicate in this matter.

Yours faithfully

Richard Baker

Figure 5. Letter to Cheap Insurance

complaints relate to claims that the repairs to the vehicle have not been carried out to a reasonable standard. *The Bulletin* published by the Insurance Ombudsman contains a summary of common complaints. A recent issue contained a summary of a complaint on the topic of repairs to a vehicle:

The policyholder's car was damaged in an accident in August and repaired by a garage approved by the insurer. At the end of the following winter, the policyholder complained about excessive paint chippings. The insurer had the car inspected by an engineer who found no evidence of defective paintwork. The policyholder had his own engineer inspect it and his opinion was that the final paint preparation was unsatisfactory. The complaint was rejected by the Ombudsman. The Ombudsman referred all the photographs and reports to an independent consultant. It was emphasised that a whole winter had passed by before the complaint had been made. In that time, the policyholder had driven some 23,000 miles. It was, therefore, impossible to conclude that the chipping and corrosion of the paintwork had been due to a substandard repair.

The Insurance Ombudsman Bureau also investigates complaints arising from other areas of insurance, such as household, medical, travel and loan protection.

Trade Associations

Trade associations can provide consumers with a way to resolve disputes. A trade association often has a code of conduct which its members are expected to observe. A consumer with a complaint against a trader who is a member can ask the association to investigate to see if the service fell below the expected standard. Many trade associations provide for an arbitration procedure to adjudicate on a complaint.

The case study involving Jeff and Sue concerns a holiday which turns out to be a disappointment. The case study is used to illustrate the possibility of using a trade association to resolve a dispute.

Case Study 17. Jeff and Sue's Holiday

Jeff and Sue go into Peaceful Tour Operators Ltd in Upmarket to book a holiday. They decide to book a 10 day holiday at the Grand Hotel on the Spanish coastal resort of Costa del Sunset. The hotel is described as top class with a swimming pool and tennis courts. The total cost is £1,400. On the first morning of their holiday, Jeff and Sue are woken up at 6am by the sound of building works next door to the hotel. This happens the next morning and they complain to the on-site tour representative. Not only is there the noise of the building work, but the dust created has made it impossible to enjoy the swimming pool. Jeff and Sue make enquiries and discover that the building work has been going on for 2 months and that Peaceful Tour Operators had sent holidaymakers during that time to the Grand Hotel. Jeff and Sue ask the tour representative for a transfer to another hotel but are told everywhere is fully booked. When they return home, they complain to the tour operator who they chose, in part, because they were members of ABTA.

It seems that Peaceful Tours Ltd were aware of the building works taking place next door. According to the ABTA Code of Conduct, they should have contacted Jeff and Sue and given them the opportunity to transfer to another holiday. Clause 2.7 of the ABTA Code states:

". . . where a tour operator becomes aware of building works which may reasonably be considered to seriously impair the enjoyment of a holiday he must, without delay, notify clients of the situation and afford them an opportunity to transfer to an alternative holiday."

When Jeff and Sue enter into correspondence with Peaceful Tours Ltd the ABTA Code of Conduct imposes time limits in which the member is expected to reply to the complaint. If Jeff and Sue are unable to resolve their dispute through correspondence with Peaceful Tours, the contract contains details of the Arbitration scheme provided by ABTA. It is a scheme devised for the travel industry by the Chartered Institute of

Arbitrators. If Jeff and Sue decide to opt for ABTA's arbitration scheme, then this will be instead of legal action and they will not be able to sue.

Under ABTA's arbitration:

- The scheme provides an inexpensive method of arbitration based on documents alone.
- The scheme does not apply for an amount greater than £1,500 per person or £7,500 per booking form.
- The client must return a completed application form to ABTA within 9 months of completing the return journey.

The Motor Industry Code of Conduct

If you have taken your car to a garage for repairs and the work has not been done to a reasonable standard, then find out if the garage is a member of a trade association. The garage may be a member of the Society of Motor Manufacturers and Traders (SMMT) or the Retail Motor Industry Federation (RMIF). These bodies have produced a code of practice. Customers who feel that the member has broken the code can apply for arbitration. The code of practice for the motor industry provides arbitration where conciliation has failed to resolve the dispute. The SMMT and the RMIF have agreed to co-operate in a low cost arbitration scheme which is organised by an independent panel of arbitrators with the decision enforceable in the County Court by either party. If the garage fails to comply with an award then the customer can apply to the court to enforce it.

The advantages of using a trade association's conciliation or arbitration scheme to settle a consumer dispute are:

- It is a relatively cheap and speedy method.
- The trader is likely to comply with the award in order to retain membership of the trade association.

The drawbacks are:

- The trader may not be a member of any association.

- There are limitations on the amount of the awards with some schemes.
- There is a suspicion in some cases that there is a bias towards the trade association member.

The Office of Fair Trading is considering the abolition of separate codes of practice which are enforced by the individual trade associations. It wants a new QUANGO to enforce a single code of conduct which would be funded by a contribution from traders who want to become members of the scheme.

Mediation

Since the mid 1980s mediation has become established in the United States and is starting to expand in this country. The Alternative Dispute Resolution Group (ADR Group), a provider of mediation, were referring only one or two cases to mediation in the early years. Just a few years later between 15 to 20 per month were going to mediation. The basis of mediation is where a third party guides both sides towards a settlement. A mediator does not make decisions or any judgment. It is the parties who eventually come to agreement between themselves.

The process involves creative problem solving with the mediator in private and confidential sessions. Then, in joint sessions, areas of agreement are drawn up and signed. In a successful mediation, the dispute is replaced by a new and binding legal agreement which ignores questions of who was right and who was wrong in law. The end result is that the original dispute is put into terms of a settlement which attempts to satisfy the interests of both parties.

The whole mediation process is "without prejudice" which means that if it fails then any admissions cannot be relied upon in any legal action. If mediation does not succeed and legal action follows, then it would have at least narrowed the areas of disagreement.

Referring a dispute to mediation can be quicker than waiting for a court hearing. It also has the benefit of not being confrontational because it does not aim to make judgments, whereas a court usually has to decide a question of fault or who was right in law. This would be of importance to someone who has a dispute with somebody with whom they regularly do business. If you are a small trader and have a dispute with an old client over a small claim, legal action may sour the relationship and could cost you future contracts. If that old client happens to be a big company which puts a considerable amount of work your way, then mediation would be an attractive method of resolving the dispute and hopefully maintaining good business relations.

An important consideration is: what does mediation cost? For low value or less complex cases where mediation will take less than half a day, it may cost around £175 per party. Where the claim is for a small amount of money, e.g. £500, this may seem a large fee. This is more than the current court fee for such a claim. However, in some circumstances, the costs may be paid by one party as part of the settlement or one party may offer to fund the entire cost of the mediation. Also, it may seem a small price to pay if it maintains an important business relationship.

Although mediation is a new concept in the legal process, the organisations that operate the scheme claim that there is a very high success rate of 95%. The ADR Group state that the success rate is that 80% of cases settle on the day and a further 10% settle within 2 weeks of the mediation.

Statutory Demands

The problem which follows, encountered by Brian Randall in the case study involving Mighty International, is familiar to many small businesses. Large companies that do not settle bills on time can cause serious problems for small traders. The small business may have suppliers chasing them for payment and so late payment seriously threatens their survival. The familiar scenario facing Brian is that Mighty International have the funds to settle the account but are taking an unreasonable time to pay. Sometimes, large organisations have a considerable number of accounts to settle, some of which are given higher priority, and so Brian is lower down the queue and therefore takes longer to receive payment.

Case Study 18. Brian and Mighty International Ltd
Brian Randall was contracted by the buildings manager of Mighty International to install some window blinds for the computer room at their head office to make it easier for VDU operators to see their screens on bright sunny days. The total cost of installing the blinds was £2,000. Brian, who is self employed, was pleased to get the order as it was larger than his usual domestic contracts. On completing the work, Brian submitted an invoice giving Mighty International 28 days to pay. At the end of this period, he sent a polite remainder that the account was overdue. He received contact from the building manager's PA to say that a cheque would arrive shortly, just as soon as she could get one signed. However, Brian has still not received payment after 2 months. Brian makes a few enquiries as to the financial state of Mighty International. He discovers that they are very profitable.

A method by which Brian could force Mighty International to settle his bill is by issuing a statutory demand. A statutory demand threatens to start proceedings to wind-up the company unless the debt is paid within 21 days. Statutory demands can also be issued against individuals. In that case, the statutory demand threatens the starting of bankruptcy proceedings against the individual if the debt is not paid.

To issue a statutory demand, the debt has to be at least £750. Also, there should be no dispute that the debt is owed. Its use is therefore appropriate in cases of late payment of invoices. Mighty International have not disputed the amount due to Brian and so a statutory demand is an option. The main benefit of a statutory demand is that the document does not have to be issued by the court and so there is no court fee to be paid. You can obtain the appropriate form from a legal stationery shop. You can also serve the document yourself. In the case of a statutory demand against a company, it should be sent to the registered office. It would be advisable to send it recorded delivery so you can prove that it was received. Where the debtor is an individual, the statutory demand must be served personally.

A statutory demand is most effective as a means to exert pressure on a company to make payment of a debt. A company that wants to continue trading will usually take notice of a statutory demand. However, it is unlikely to be worth the creditor starting winding-up or bankruptcy proceedings unless the debt is of a substantial size.

If the debtor fails to respond to the statutory demand then you have to decide whether or not to begin winding-up or bankruptcy proceedings. To start such proceedings, the creditor has to:

- File a petition at the court.
- Pay a court fee.
- Lodge a sizeable deposit for the Official Receiver.

The cost is expensive. The Official Receiver's deposit is several hundred pounds for a bankruptcy petition and even more for winding-up proceedings. It might seem a hollow threat when you issue a statutory demand but the debtor will not know whether you will follow up with a petition to wind-up, or make bankrupt, as a matter of principle. Therefore, this possibility will hopefully persuade the debtor to pay.

The Media
In recent years, there has been a growth of radio and television programmes devoted to consumer issues. These programmes investigate alleged unfairness and poor customer service in order to expose it to other consumers and obviously to attract viewers and listeners. While it is not suggested that every time you have a consumer dispute you should approach the media, sometimes a well written letter to a newspaper or programme maker may suddenly produce an unexpected offer to settle. Obviously, one of the reasons to settle may be the wish to

avoid any bad publicity. One should, however, be cautious of investigative reporters wishing to expose an alleged consumer injustice. Television reporters have a duty to make programmes which will interest viewers and so some might be tempted to spice up the facts. It might produce an offer to settle, but, equally, it might antagonise the company and so make a compromise impossible. If you do decide to highlight your plight by writing to a newspaper, make sure you stick to the facts, because you do not want to be sued for libel.

10

MAKING A CLAIM BEFORE THE CIVIL JUSTICE REFORMS

- Introduction
- The Rules Before the Reform

Introduction

Lord Woolf undertook a comprehensive reform of the civil justice system which considered ways of improving the operation of the civil courts. He addressed the time it took for cases to be heard, the cost of legal action and the simplification of the court rules. One of the main reforms was to establish three different tracks within the court system to which cases would be allocated, depending on the size and nature of the claim. As part of this three track system, the small claims procedure was increased in importance so that cases are referred to the small claims track where the financial value is not more than £5,000. Before the implementation of these reforms the small claims limit was £3,000. When changes are made to the legal system, there is usually a transition period when the old rules will continue to apply. This chapter outlines the important differences in the rules for making a small claim under the old system in case you started your action before 26th April 1999 when the new rules took effect.

The Rules Before the Reform

Before the Woolf reforms, a claim would be started by issuing a summons. A summons was the equivalent of the claim form and the details on a summons were much the same as those now required on a claim form – the parties to the action, the nature and the amount of the claim. Before the reforms, the person making a claim was referred to as the ''plaintiff''. The lay person was often confused by this term and the person bringing the claim is now called the ''claimant''. There were two types of summons:

- A default summons.
- A fixed date summons.

A default summons was used when claiming an amount of money and the fixed date summons was where the remedy was for something other than money, for example recovering the possession of goods. To complicate things further, there were two types of default summons. There was a form of summons where the claim was for a fixed amount of money (for example, a straightforward debt action for unpaid invoices), and another type of summons where the amount was not fixed (such as damages for personal injury where the court would decide the appropriate level of compensation). The two types of default summons are illustrated in Appendix B.

Under the old rules, when a court served the summons by 1st class post on the defendant, the date of service was on the seventh day after posting, in the case of individuals, and the second working day after posting in the case of companies. The defendant had 14 days from the date of service in which to respond to the summons. That is different from the new rules, where, provided a notice of intention to defend is filed within 14 days of service, the defendant has 28 days from the date of service of the claim in which to file a defence.

If the defendant filed a defence under the old rules, you did not receive an allocation questionnaire which now happens. It would have been allocated to the small claims procedure and a date set for the arbitration. The standard directions sent out required the plaintiff to exchange all documents they were to rely on at least 14 days before the hearing, and any experts' reports or witness statements at least 7 days before the hearing with copies to be filed at court. Before the reforms, it was not necessary to seek the permission of the court to use expert evidence either in written or oral form. If you now wish to use expert evidence you have to indicate your intention to do so on the allocation questionnaire.

If you issued a summons under the old rules for a liquidated sum, the case would automatically transfer to the defendant's home court on the filing of a defence. This happened if the defendant was an individual or company. Under the new rules, there would not be the automatic transfer where the defendant is a company.

APPENDIX A

OFFICIAL FORMS
Claim Form
Request for Oral Examination (N316)
Request for Warrant of Execution (N323)
Request for Attachment of Earnings Order (N337)
Affidavit in Support of Application for Garnishee Order
(N349)

Crown copyright is reproduced with the permission of the
Controller of Her Majesty's Stationery Office.

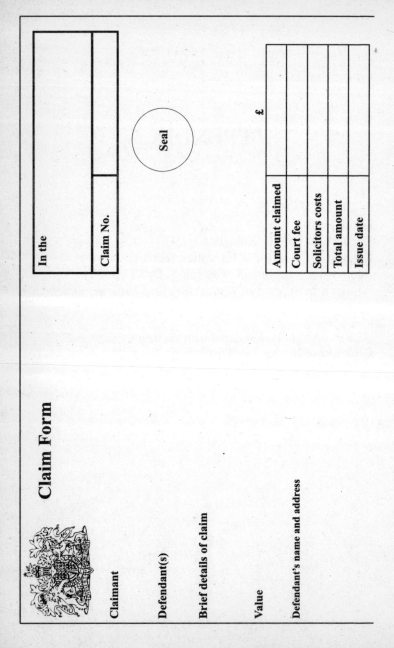

Claim Form

Claimant

Defendant(s)

Brief details of claim

Value

Defendant's name and address

In the

Claim No.

Seal

	£
Amount claimed	
Court fee	
Solicitors costs	
Total amount	
Issue date	

Particulars of claim (attached)(to follow)

Statement of Truth

*(I believe)(The Claimant believes) that the facts stated in these particulars of claim are true.

* I am duly authorised by the claimant to sign this statement

Full name _____

Name of claimant's solicitor's firm _____

signed _____ position or office held _____

*(Claimant)(Litigation friend)(Claimant's solicitor) (if signing on behalf of firm or company)

*delete as appropriate

Claimant or claimant's solicitor's address to which documents or payments should be sent if different from overleaf. If you are prepared to accept service by DX, fax or e-mail, please add details.

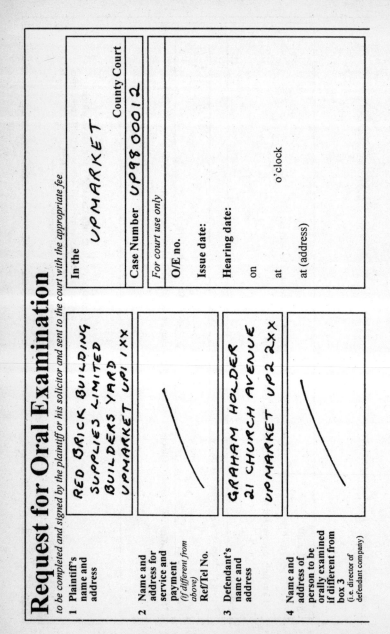

Request for Oral Examination

to be completed and signed by the plaintiff or his solicitor and sent to the court with the appropriate fee

In the

UPMARKET

County Court

Case Number UP98 00012

For court use only

O/E no.

Issue date:

Hearing date:

on

at   o'clock

at (address)

1 Plaintiff's name and address

RED BRICK BUILDING
SUPPLIES LIMITED
BUILDERS YARD
UPMARKET UP1 1XX

2 Name and address for service and payment
(if different from above)
Ref/Tel No.

3 Defendant's name and address

GRAHAM HOLDER
21 CHURCH AVENUE
UPMARKET UP2 2XX

4 Name and address of person to be orally examined if different from box 3
(i.e. director of defendant company)

5 Judgment details

Court where judgment/order
made if not court of issue

6 Outstanding debt

*you may be able
to claim interest
if judgment
entered for more
than £5000 on or
after 1 July 1991

Balance of debt and any interest*/damages at date of this request	1580	—
Issue fee	30	—
AMOUNT NOW DUE	1610	—
Unsatisfied warrant costs		

I apply for an order that the above defendant (the officer of the defendant company named in Box 4) attend and be orally examined as to his (the defendant company's) financial circumstances and produce at the examination any relevant books or documents

I certify that the balance now due is as shown

Signed   *Red Brick Building Supplies Ltd*

Plaintiff (~~Plaintiff's solicitor~~)

Dated xx/xx/xx

IMPORTANT

**You must inform the court immediately of any payments you
receive after you have sent this request to the court**

N316   Request for oral examination (Order 25, rule 3(1A))

Request for Warrant of Execution

to be completed and signed by the plaintiff or his solicitor and sent to the court with the appropriate fee

1 Plaintiff's name and address

RED BRICK BUILDING
SUPPLIES LIMITED
BUILDERS YARD
UPMARKET UP11 XX

2 Name and address for service and payment *(if different from above)* **Ref/Tel No.**

3 Defendant's name and address

GRAHAM HOLDER
21 CHURCH AVENUE
UPMARKET
UP2 2XX

In the UPMARKET County Court

Case Number UP9800012

For court use only

Warrant no.

Issue date:

Warrant applied for at   o'clock

Foreign court code/name:

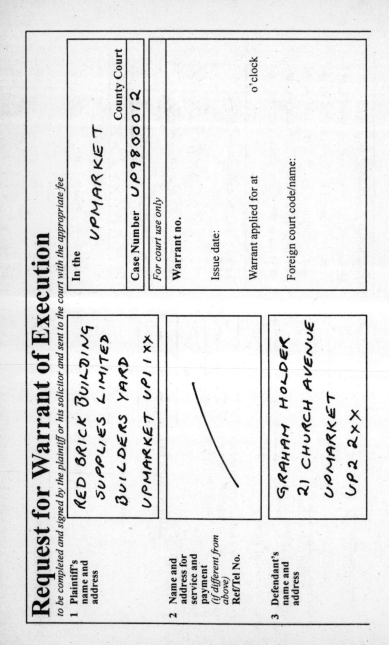

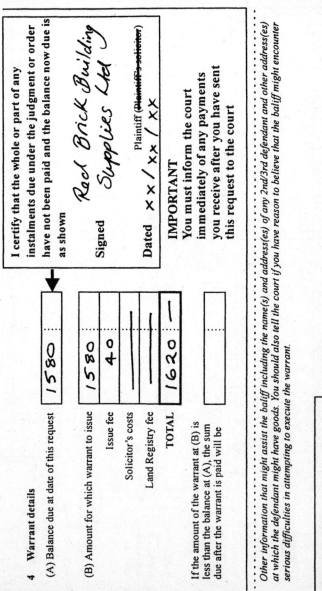

4 Warrant details

(A) Balance due at date of this request

| 1580 |

(B) Amount for which warrant to issue

	1580
Issue fee	40
Solicitor's costs	—
Land Registry fee	—
TOTAL	1620 —

If the amount of the warrant at (B) is less than the balance at (A), the sum due after the warrant is paid will be

I certify that the whole or part of any instalments due under the judgment or order have not been paid and the balance now due is as shown

Signed *Red Brick Building Supplies Ltd*

Dated xx / xx / xx

Plaintiff (~~Plaintiff's Solicitor~~)

IMPORTANT
You must inform the court immediately of any payments you receive after you have sent this request to the court

Other information that might assist the baliff including the name(s) and address(es) of any 2nd/3rd defendant and other address(es) at which the defendant might have goods. You should also tell the court if you have reason to believe that the baliff might encounter serious difficulties in attempting to execute the warrant.

Warrant No.

N 323

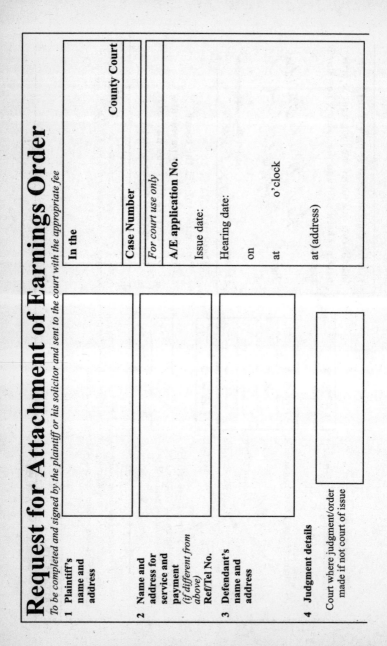

5 Outstanding debt

Balance due at date of this request* (excluding issue fee but including unsatisfied warrant costs)

Issue fee

AMOUNT NOW DUE

* you may also be entitled to interest to date of request where judgment over £5000 and entered on or after 1 July 1991

6 Employment details

(please give as much information as you can – it will help the court to make an order more quickly)

Employer's name and address

Defendant's place of work *(if different from employer's address)*

The defendant is employed as

Works No/Pay Ref

I apply for an attachment of earnings order

I certify that the whole or part of any instalments due under the judgment or order have not been paid and the balance now due is as shown

Signed

Plaintiff (Plaintiff's solicitor)

Dated

7 Other details
(Give any other details about the defendant's circumstances which may be relevant to the application)

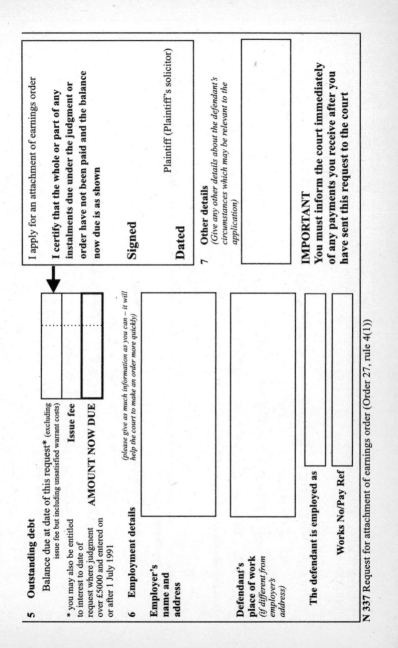

IMPORTANT
You must inform the court immediately of any payments you receive after you have sent this request to the court

N 337 Request for attachment of earnings order (Order 27, rule 4(1))

Affidavit in support of application for Garnishee Order
Order 30, rule 2

In the UPMARKET   County Court

           UP9800012   Case No

BETWEEN REDBRICK BUILDING SUPPLIES LIMITED   Plaintiff Creditor

AND GRAHAM HOLDER   Defendant

AND UPMARKET BANK PLC   Garnishee

1,(1) RED BRICK BUILDING SUPPLIES LIMITED

[~~Solicitor for~~] the above-named plaintiff make oath and say:—

1. That [I] [   ] on the XX   day of XX   (year)

obtained a [judgment] [~~an order~~] in this court against the above-named defendant for payment of the sum of £1,580 for [debt] [~~damages~~] and costs.

2. That £1,580 is still due and unpaid under the [judgment] [~~order~~].

3. That to the best of my information or belief the garnishee,

of UPMARKET HIGH STREET, UPMARKET

is indebted to the defendant [in the sum of £4,000   ]. [(2) The grounds of my information or belief are: (3)

AN ORAL EXAMINATION

1

4. That the garnishee is a deposit-taking institution having more than one place of business [and the name and address of the branch at which the defendant's account is believed to be held is UPMARKET HIGH STREET, UPMARKET]

and the number of the account is believed to be 00245654

[I do not know at which branch the defendant's account is held, or what the number of the account is].

5. That the last known address for the defendant is 21 CHURCH AVENUE UPMARKET UP2 2XX

SWORN at UPMARKET COUNTY COURT

in the COUNTY of UPMARKET SHIRE

this XX day of XX (year)

Before me,

C. Smith

(C. SMITH)

OFFICER OF A COURT, APPOINTED BY
THE JUDGE TO TAKE AFFIDAVITS.

This Affidavit is filed on behalf of the plaintiff.
(1) Insert full name, address and occupation of deponent
(2) Add if known
(3) State your grounds

Delete any words in square brackets which do not apply

N349

APPENDIX B

SUMMONS (PRE-REFORM)
Default Summons (fixed amount) (N1)
Default Summons (amount not fixed) (N2)

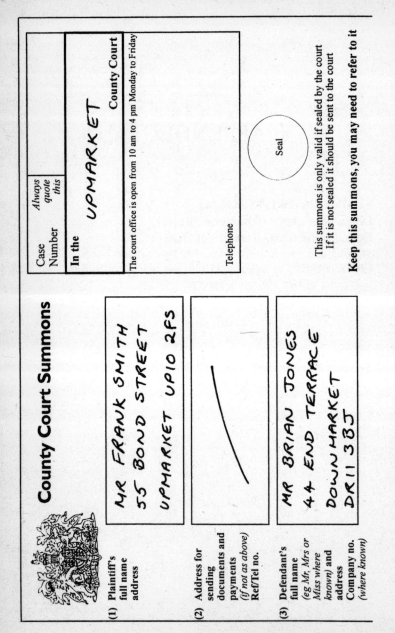

County Court Summons

| Case Number | *Always quote this* |

In the *UPMARKET*

County Court

The court office is open from 10 am to 4 pm Monday to Friday

Telephone

Seal

This summons is only valid if sealed by the court
If it is not sealed it should be sent to the court

Keep this summons, you may need to refer to it

(1) Plaintiff's full name address

*MR FRANK SMITH
55 BOND STREET
UPMARKET UP10 2FS*

(2) Address for sending documents and payments *(if not as above)* Ref/Tel no.

(3) Defendant's full name *(eg Mr, Mrs or Miss where known)* and address Company no. *(where known)*

*MR BRIAN JONES
44 END TERRACE
DOWNMARKET
DR11 3BJ*

What the plaintiff claims from you

Amount claimed	506	14
Court fee	60	—
Solicitor's costs		
Total amount	**566**	**14**
Summons issued on		

Brief
description of type of claim | ROAD TRAFFIC CLAIM

Particulars of the plaintiff's claim against you

SEE ATTACHED

PARTICULARS OF CLAIM

Signed *Frank Smith*

Plaintiff's ~~solicitor~~
(or see enclosed particulars of claim)

N1 Default summons (fixed amount) (Order 3, rule 3(2)(b))

What to do about this summons
You have 21 days from the date of the postmark to reply to this summons
(A limited company served at its registered office has 16 days to reply)
If this summons was delivered by hand, you have 14 days from the date it was delivered to reply

You can
• dispute the claim
• make a claim against the plaintiff
• admit the claim and costs in full and offer to pay
• admit only part of the claim
• pay the total amount shown above

You must read the information on the back of this form. It will tell you more about what to do.

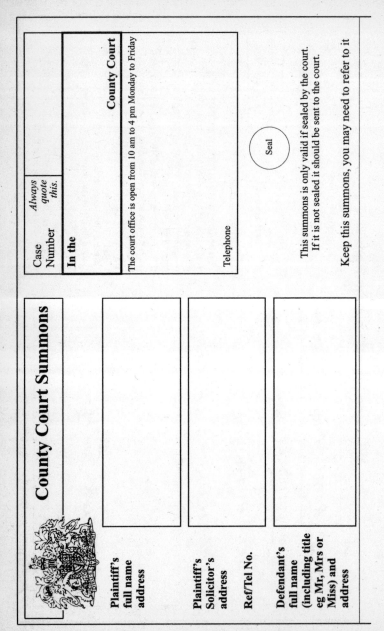

County Court Summons

Plaintiff's full name address

Plaintiff's Solicitor's address

Ref/Tel No.

Defendant's full name (including title eg Mr, Mrs or Miss) and address

Case Number | *Always quote this.*

In the   **County Court**

The court office is open from 10 am to 4 pm Monday to Friday

Telephone

Seal

This summons is only valid if sealed by the court. If it is not sealed it should be sent to the court.

Keep this summons, you may need to refer to it

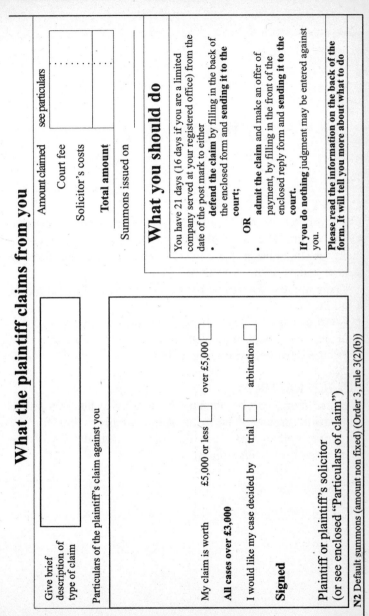

What the plaintiff claims from you

Amount claimed	see particulars
Court fee	
Solicitor's costs	
Total amount	

Summons issued on

What you should do

You have 21 days (16 days if you are a limited company served at your registered office) from the date of the post mark to either

- **defend the claim** by filling in the back of the enclosed form and **sending it to the court;**

OR

- **admit the claim** and make an offer of payment, by filling in the front of the enclosed reply form and **sending it to the court.**

If you do nothing judgment may be entered against you.

Please read the information on the back of the form. It will tell you more about what to do

---

Give brief description of type of claim

Particulars of the plaintiff's claim against you

My claim is worth   £5,000 or less ☐   over £5,000 ☐

All cases over £3,000

I would like my case decided by   trial ☐   arbitration ☐

Signed

Plaintiff or plaintiff's solicitor
(or see enclosed "Particulars of claim")

N2 Default summons (amount non fixed) (Order 3, rule 3(2)(b))

APPENDIX C

COUNTY COURT FEES

The level of the court fee to issue a claim depends on the size of the claim. Therefore, the larger the claim the higher the court fee. In addition, there may be other fees you have to pay at later stages in the procedure.

There are also fees to be paid for each method of enforcing a judgment.

Court fees are liable to change from time to time and so it is vital that you check with your local County Court as to the appropriate fee before issuing a claim.

POLICE REPORT

A police report can be obtained by writing to the area police administration unit. The Area Administrative Unit for the particular police force will be able to give details of the current fee for a police report.

APPENDIX D

USEFUL ADDRESSES AND CONTACTS

Consumer Organisations
Consumers' Association Ltd
2 Marylebone Road
LONDON NW1 4DF
Tel. 0171 830 6000   Fax. 0171 830 7600

Ombudsmen
Banking Ombudsman
70 Grays Inn Road
LONDON WC1X 8NB
Tel. 0171 404 9944

Independent Housing Ombudsman
Norman House
105-109 The Strand
LONDON WC2R 0AA
Tel. 0345 125973   Fax. 0171 836 3900

Insurance Ombudsman
City Gate One
135 Park Street
LONDON SE1 9EA
Tel. 0845 600 6666

Legal Services Ombudsman
22 Oxford Court
Oxford Street
MANCHESTER M2 3WQ
Tel. 0161 236 9532   Fax. 0161 236 2651

Trade Associations
Cars:
Retail Motor Industry Federation Ltd
201 Great Portland Street
LONDON W1N 6AB

Society of Motor Manufacturers and Traders Limited
Forbes House
Halkin Street
LONDON SW1X 7DS

Double Glazing:
Glass and Glazing Federation
44-48 Borough High Street
LONDON SE1 1XB

Electrical Goods:
The Association of Manufacturers of Domestic & Electrical
Appliances
Rapier House
40-46 Lambs Conduit
LONDON WC1N 3NW

Travel:
Association of British Travel Agents
68-71 Newham Street
LONDON W1P 4AH

Miscellaneous
Equifax Plc
Dolphin House
PO Box 61
New Street
SALISBURY SP1 2TB
Tel. 01722 413434

This company will conduct a search to discover whether or not a vehicle is on hire purchase, is recorded stolen or has been registered a write-off.

Alternative Dispute Resolution Group (A.D.R. Group)
Grove House
Grove Road
Redland
BRISTOL BS6 6UN
Tel. 0117 946 7180   Fax. 0117 946 7181

A.D.R. Group provides mediation services.

Registry Trust Ltd
173-175 Cleveland Street
LONDON W1P 5PE
Tel. 0171 380 0133

The Registry Trust maintains a register of all County Court judgments. The register can be searched by sending a fee of £4.50.

Companies Registration Office
Companies House
Crown Way
CARDIFF CF4 3UZ
Tel. 01222 380801

The registered office of a limited company registered in

England & Wales can be obtained through contacting the Companies Registration Office.

Customer Enquiries (Vehicles) Unit
DVLA
SWANSEA
SA99 1BN
Tel. 01792 772134 (Vehicle Enquiries)

Customer Enquiries (Drivers) Unit
DVLA
SWANSEA
SA6 7JL
Tel. 01792 772151 (Driver Enquiries)

The name and address of the registered keeper of a motor vehicle can be obtained by sending a written request to the DVLA stating the reason you require the information and a cheque for £3.50.

Motor Insurers' Bureau
152 Silbury Boulevard
CENTRAL MILTON KEYNES
MK9 1NB
Tel. 01908 240000

The Defence Council
The Ministry of Defence
Whitehall
LONDON SW1

INDEX

A
Affidavit, 68–69, 115–116
Allocation questionnaire, 12–13, 96
Appeal, right of, 104
Arbitration, 7, 8–9, 10, 76, 92 *et seq.*
Attachment of earnings order,
    112–114
Automatic transfer, 63–64, 75–76

C
Charging order, 115–117
Claim form, 50–51
    , responses to the, 70–78
Claimant, 51, 135
Consent order, 72–73, 99
Consumer claim, 33–38, 59–61,
    84–89
    Credit Act, 24
Contract, 20 *et seq.*
    terms, express, 20
    , implied, 20–21
    , unfair, 22
Contributory negligence, 26
Costs, 54, 103–104
Counterclaim, 79, 83–84, 87
County Court, 11–12
Court fees (see Appendix C)
    , payment of, 64

D
Defence, 79 *et seq.*
Defendant's details, 52–54
Dishonoured cheque, 87–89

Documents, 92–93, 95 *et seq.,* 100
Duty of care, 19–20

E
Enforcing judgment, 46, 106 *et seq.*
Enquiry agent, 67–68, 108

F
Faulty goods (see Consumer claim)
Financial status report, 47–48
Form of Reply, 65

G
Garnishee order, 114–115

H
Hearing (see Arbitration)
Highway claim, 41–44, 90–91
Highways Act 1980, 90

I
Injunction, 103
Interest on claim, 54–55

J
Judgment in default, 11, 76–78
    set aside, 78

L
Landlord/tenant disputes, 61–63
Legal basis of claims, 18, 19 *et seq*
Letter before action, 35 *et seq.*
    (see also without prejudice letters)

M
Media, 132–133
Mediation, 129–130
Minor in court action, 53
Misrepresentation, 21, 22–23

N
Negligence, 19 *et seq.*
Negotiation, 31–35
"No costs" rule, 8, 49, 98
Non-attendance, 105
Notice of Issue form, 65, 72

O
Ombudsmen, 122–126, 155–156
Opening statement, 100–101
Oral examination, 107–109,
   110–111

P
Particulars of claim, 36, 50, 55–63
Personal injury claims, 15–16
Plaintiff, 135
Pre-Woolf, 8, 134 *et seq.*

Q
Questions for the defendant,
   102–103

R
Reasonable man, 20
Register of County Court
   judgments, 47, 107
Repair of faulty goods, 34–35
Representation, 98, 100

Road traffic claim, 25–26, 38–41,
   56–59, 80–84

S
Satisfactory quality, 27–30
Serving the claim form, 65–71
Small Claims Court, 10 *et seq.*
Specific performance claims,
   15–16, 103
Statutory demand, 46, 130–132
Suing, basic checks before, 47–48
   , capacity in which you are,
   51–52
Summons, 134–135

T
Tort, 18
Trade associations, 126–129, 156

U
Uninsured driver, 45
Unpaid judgments, 119

V
Vexatious litigant, 8

W
Warrant of execution, 46, 104,
   111–112
Warranty claims, 23–24
Where to bring your claim, 63–64
Without prejudice letters, 33
Witnesses, 95 *et seq.*
Woolf reforms, 10–11, 134
   (see also Pre-Woolf)
   Report, 8, 121

FREE